Vintage Hollywood Posters II

Day of Sale
Saturday, June 26, 1999
4:00 p.m.

Feldman Gallery
PACIFIC DESIGN CENTER
8687 Melrose Avenue
West Hollywood, California

Exhibition
Sunday, June 20, 2:00 p.m. - 6:00 p.m.
Monday, June 21, 10:30 a.m. - 5:30 p.m.
Tuesday, June 22, 10:30 a.m. - 5:30 p.m.
at the
HOWARD LOWERY GALLERY
3812 W. Magnolia Boulevard
Burbank, California 91505
and
Thursday, June 24, 11:00 a.m. - 8:00 p.m.
Friday, June 25, 11:00 a.m. - 8:00 p.m.
Saturday, June 26, 10:00 a.m. - 12:00 noon
at the
Feldman Gallery
PACIFIC DESIGN CENTER

HOWARD LOWERY GALLERY
3812 W. Magnolia Boulevard, Burbank, California 91505

Telephone: (818) 972-9080   Fax: (818) 972-3910

Conditions of Sale

The following conditions and other information printed in this catalogue constitute the entire terms and conditions under which Howard Lowery (hereinafter "Lowery") will offer and sell the property described herein. In conducting this auction Lowery acts solely as the agent of the seller or consignor of the property offered for sale. By placing a bid in this auction, whether in person, through an agent, by telephone, by mail, or by any other means, the buyer agrees to be bound by these conditions of sale.

1. Conduct of the Sale.

a) The buyer for each lot shall be the highest bidder recognized by and acceptable to Lowery. In the event of a dispute during the auction, Lowery may, at his sole and absolute discretion, either determine the identity of the highest bidder, re-offer the lot for sale, or withdraw the lot from the sale. In the event of a dispute after the auction Lowery's sale records shall be conclusive in all respects.

b) Lowery, as auctioneer, shall determine opening bids and bidding increments. Lowery reserves the right to withdraw any lot prior to its sale. Lowery may execute bids for absentee bidders as set forth in the following "Procedures for Bidding."

c) All lots are sold subject to reserve prices which are the confidential minimum prices below which the lots will not be sold. Lowery or his representative may bid on each lot up to the reserve price. Consignors may not bid on their own items beyond the reserve price.

d) Bidders are deemed to be acting as principals unless Lowery acknowledges in writing prior to the auction that the bidder is acting as an agent for another party. Unless such acknowledgment is made all bidders guarantee payment of full purchase price for all successful bids.

e) All successful bidders agree to confirm their bids in writing upon request.

f) Lowery reserves the right to refuse to accept bids from anyone.

2. Responsibility for Purchased Lots.

Full risk and responsibility for each lot passes to the buyer at the time he or she is declared to be the highest bidder by the auctioneer. Thereafter, neither Lowery nor any of his agents or employees shall be liable for any loss or damage to the property.

3. Purchase Price and Payment Terms.

a) For each lot for which the buyer is the highest bidder, the buyer shall pay the full purchase price to Lowery, which shall consist of the final bid price plus a buyer's premium, as set forth below, and any applicable sales tax.

b) For each lot the buyer's premium shall be 15% of the final bid price. Cash, approved check or money order are accepted for payment. Credit cards will not be accepted for payment in this auction.

c) All amounts and payments shall be in U.S. dollars.

d) If payment is made by personal or business check, delivery of property purchased shall be delayed until the check has cleared the bank.

e) Payment in full may be made during or after the auction. Subsequent to the day of the auction payment in full is due at Lowery's business address (3812 W. Magnolia Blvd., Burbank, CA 91505) within 10 calendar days of the auction. Business hours are 10:30 a.m. - 5:30 p.m., Tuesday through Saturday.

f) For absentee bidders only, payment in full must be made within seven calendar days after receipt by the buyer of Lowery's written invoice.

4. Remedies for Non-Payment

a) In the event the buyer fails to comply with the foregoing payment terms, Lowery, at his sole and absolute discretion may
  1) seek to collect payment and damages by all legal means,
  2) cancel the sale.

b) In the event such action is necessary, Lowery may retain as liquidated damages any and all payment made by the buyer or amounts owed by Lowery to the buyer to the extent of the full purchase price.

5. Collection of Purchased Lots

Property will be delivered to the buyer upon receipt by Lowery of the full purchase price at the site of the auction or at Lowery's business address (3812 W. Magnolia Blvd., Burbank, CA 91505). In the event buyer requests shipment to his or her address, Lowery or his designated agent will, at his discretion, undertake packaging and shipping services as an accommodation to the buyer. Under no circumstances will Lowery or his employees or agents be held liable for any damage to or loss of the property or for delay in delivery. The buyer agrees to pay such shipping and handling fees charged by Lowery or his agent.

6. Warranties.

a) All descriptions, illustrations, and terminology used in this catalogue represent a full effort made in good faith by Lowery to accurately represent the lots offered for sale as to origin, date, condition, and other information contained therein. Price estimates are provided solely as a guide to prospective buyers and are not intended as representations of actual values or predictions of final bid prices. All items, however, are sold "as is," and Lowery makes no express or implied warranties as to merchantability, authenticity or condition of any lot or of the correctness of the description of any lot. Prospective bidders are urged to inspect the lots personally or otherwise satisfy themselves as to the nature of each lot.

b) In the event Lowery is prevented by fire, theft or any other reason from delivering any property to the buyer, any liability of Lowery shall be limited to the amount actually paid for the property by the buyer.

c) No warranty or representation is made to the buyer that he or she acquires any copyright or reproduction rights by purchasing any lot in this auction.

7. Governing Law.

By placing a bid in the auction all buyers consent to be governed by laws of the State of California and agree that any actions arising under the terms of the auction will be determined by courts in Los Angeles County, California. This auction is conducted pursuant to California law. Howard Lowery is bonded to the State of California, office of the Secretary of State, Sacramento, California.

8. Attorney's Fees.

In the event legal action is required to enforce any of the terms contained herein the prevailing party shall be entitled to recover attorney's fees.

Procedures for Bidding

1. Bids will be accepted by mail, telephone, or in person at Lowery's business address (3812 W. Magnolia Blvd, Burbank, CA 91505) prior to the day of sale (June 26, 1999) as follows:

a) Mail, Fax or In-Person Bids. Written bids using Lowery's bid form must be received no later than 6:00 p.m. on Thursday, June 24, 1999. Bids will be executed by Lowery on behalf of the bidder up to, but not exceeding, the amount of the written bid for each lot. This service is offered as a convenience to "absentee bidders" and neither Lowery nor his agents nor employees shall be held liable for the failure to execute such bids. Identical bids for the same lot shall be executed in favor of the bid with the earliest postmark.

b) Telephone Bids. By prior arrangement, during the auction Lowery or his agents or employees will attempt to telephone prospective bidders who cannot attend the auction and allow them to place bids by telephone. Prospective telephone bidders must submit to Lowery a completed and signed bid sheet (enclosed with this catalogue) listing lots in which they are interested by 6:00 p.m. on Thursday, June 24, 1999.

The number of persons who can be telephoned to bid for a particular lot is limited. In the event more persons request to be telephoned than can be accommodated, Lowery reserves the right to contact those persons prior to the auction to determine their individual levels of interest and to decide who will be called during the auction by conducting pre-auction bidding.

Although a good faith effort will be made to reach such bidders, Lowery will not be held liable in the event that such efforts are unsuccessful. Prospective bidders are urged to make themselves available to receive telephone calls during the auction. This service is offered as a convenience to "absentee bidders" and neither Lowery nor his agents nor employees shall be held liable for the failure to execute such bids.

3. Bids will also be accepted prior to the auction in person by Lowery or his representative at Feldman Gallery of the Pacific Design Center, 8687 Melrose Avenue, West Hollywood, California 90069 during exhibition hours on Thursday, June 24.

4. Bidders who attend the auction must register with the receptionist and have in their possession a bid number issued by Lowery in order to bid. Possession of a catalogue will admit two persons to the auction. Catalogues may be purchased at the auction site.

5. This auction will be held at Feldman Gallery of the Pacific Design Center, 8687 Melrose Avenue, West Hollywood, California 90069. Registration will commence at 2:00 pm; the auction will start at 4:00 pm.

The original country of origin posters from classic non-U.S. films are very desirable. They are often rarer than, and have superior artwork to, the U.S. posters from the same titles.

1. La Dolce Vita, Cineriz, 1960, Italian poster, Cond. B+, linenbacked, 78 x 55 in $5,000-7000

2. La Dolce Vita, Cineriz, 1960, Italian poster, Cond. B+, linenbacked, 78 x 55 in $1,500-2,500

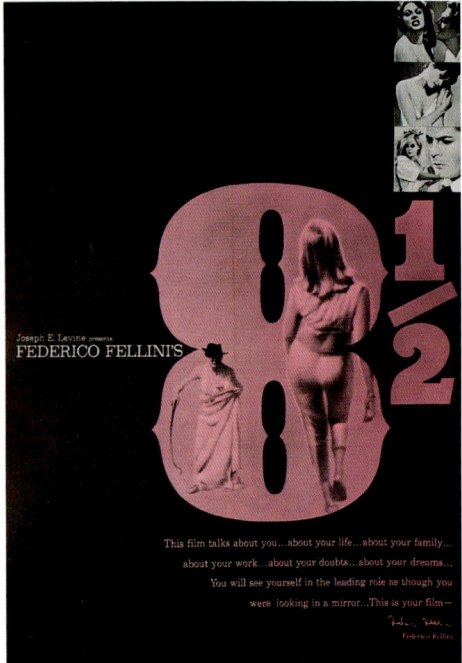

3. Eight and a Half, Embassy, 1963, one-sheet, Cond. B+, linenbacked, 41 x 27 in $200-400

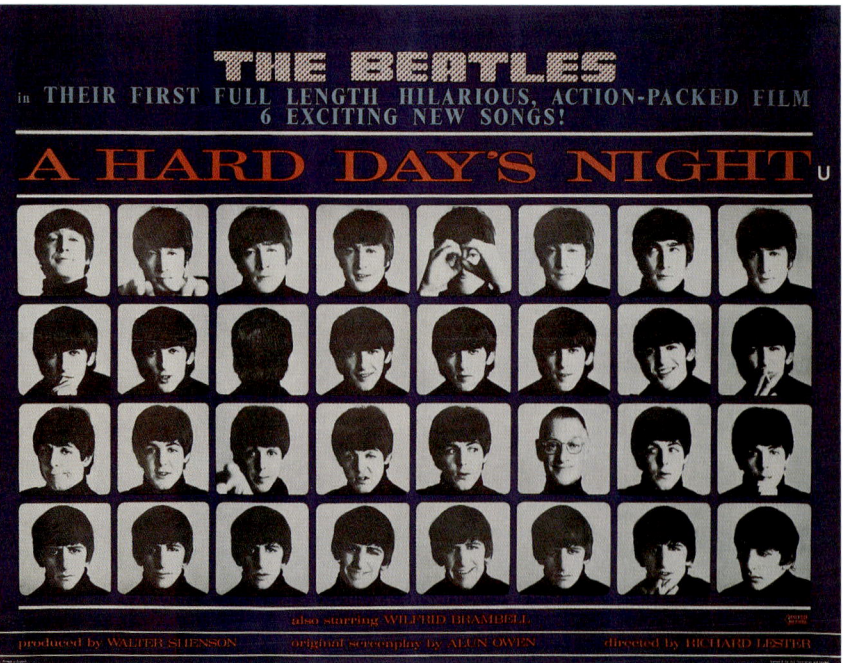

4. A Hard Day's Night, United Artists, 1964, British quad, Cond. B+, linenbacked, 30 x 40 in $800-1,200

Many of the best posters of the 1960s have become difficult to obtain in recent years, as baby boomers seem most attracted to those films that they grew up with.

5. 2001: a space odyssey, MGM, 1968, three-sheet, Cond. B+, linenbacked, 81 x 41 in $800-1,200

6. 2001: a space odyssey, MGM, 1968, British quad, Cond. A-, 30 x 40 in $600-800

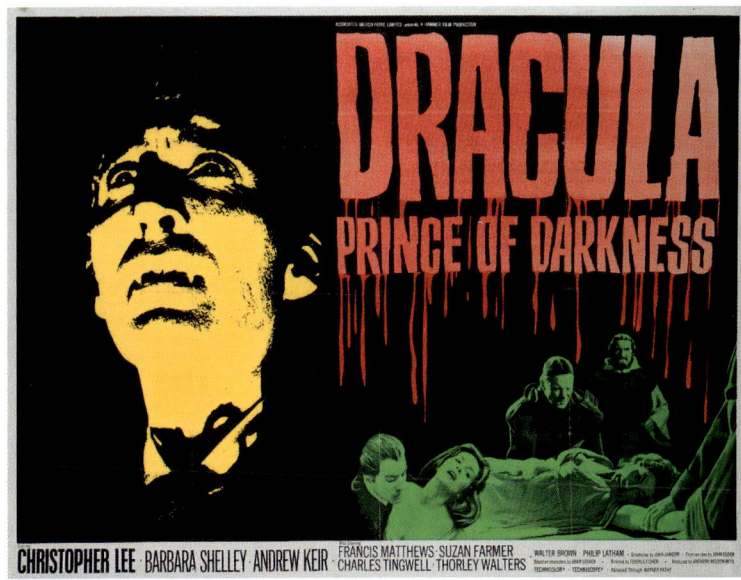

7. Dracula Prince of Darkness, Warner-Pathe, 1965, British quad, Cond. B+, 30 x 40 in $200-400

8. Ocean's 11, Warner Brothers, 1960, one-sheet, Cond. B+, linenbacked, 41 x 27 in $700-900

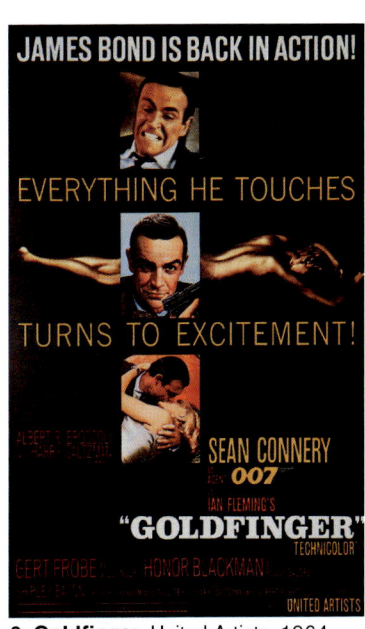

9. Goldfinger, United Artists, 1964, one-sheet, Cond. B, linenbacked, 41 x 27 in $700-900

10. From Russia With Love, United Artists, 1964, one-sheet, Cond. A-, 41 x 27 in $300-500

Steve Reeves was the prototype for later action stars such as Bruce Lee. Steve McQueen was the epitomy of "cool" through all his many memorable roles.

11. Enter the Dragon, Warner Brothers, 1973, six-sheet, Cond. A-, linenbacked, 81 x 81 in $800-1,200

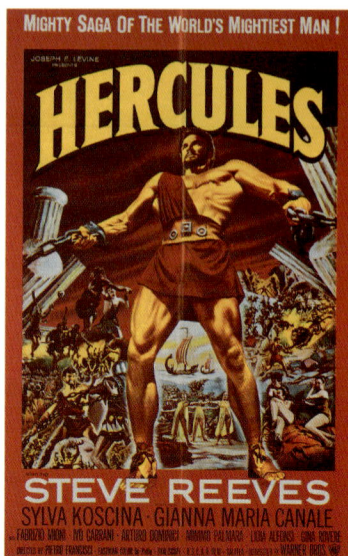

12. Hercules, Warner Brothers, 1959, one-sheet, Cond. A, 41 x 27 in
$100-200

13. The Great Escape, United Artists, 1963, one-sheet, Cond. B+, 41 x 27 in $400-600

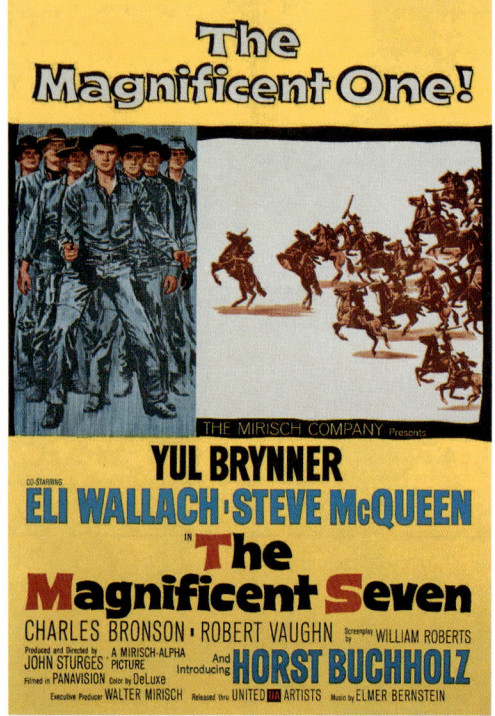

14. The Magnificent Seven, United Artists, 1960, one-sheet, Cond. B, linenbacked, 41 x 27 in
$400-600

15. Bullitt, Warner Brothers, 1968, advance one-sheet, Cond. B+, linenbacked, 41 x 27 in $200-400

16. Le Mans, National General, 1971, one-sheet, Cond. A-, 41 x 27 in $75-150

The best posters of the 1960s and 1970s have understandably been rising in popularity in the last few years, and the most desired of these are from the most memorable films of that era.

17. The Hustler, 20th Century Fox, 1964 reissue, one-sheet, Cond. A, 41 x 27 in $300-500

18. Midnight Cowboy, United Artists, 1969, one-sheet, Cond. B+, 41 x 27 in $75-150

19. The Deer Hunter, EMI, 1978, British one-sheet, Cond. A, unfolded, 40 x 27 in $500-700

20. Star Wars, 20th Century Fox, 1977, style C one-sheet, Cond. A, 41 x 27 in $150-300

21. Star Wars, 20th Century Fox, 1977, style A one-sheet, Cond. A, 41 x 27 in $100-200

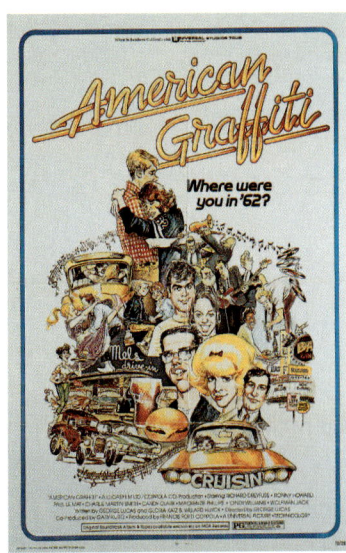

22. American Graffiti, Universal, 1973, one-sheet, Cond. A-, 41 x 27 in $100-200

23. The Endless Summer, Cinema V, 1966, one-sheet, Cond. B+, 41 x 27 in $400-600

24. Manhattan, United Artists, 1979, one-sheet, Cond. A-, 41 x 27 in $75-150

25. The Sting, Universal, 1973, one-sheet, Cond. B+, 41 x 27 in $75-150

Snow White and the Seven Dwarfs was released in February of 1938, but, as many films do, it had a premiere in Los Angeles in late December of 1937. Consequently, some of the posters are dated 1937 and some are dated 1938. Offered on this and the following three pages is the finest collection of Snow White material ever assembled. It includes items never before offered in any venue.

26. Snow White and the Seven Dwarfs, Walt Disney, 1938, style C one-sheet, Cond. A-, unfolded, 41 x 27 in $10,000-15,000

Most films have either one or two different styles of one-sheets, although studios would sometimes create more than two styles for major films. For **Snow White**, a special C style one-sheet was made, in both a regular folded version on thin paper, and a deluxe unfolded version, on heavy stock that has a linen-like finish. The B style shows all the major characters, while the A style just depicts the dwarfs.

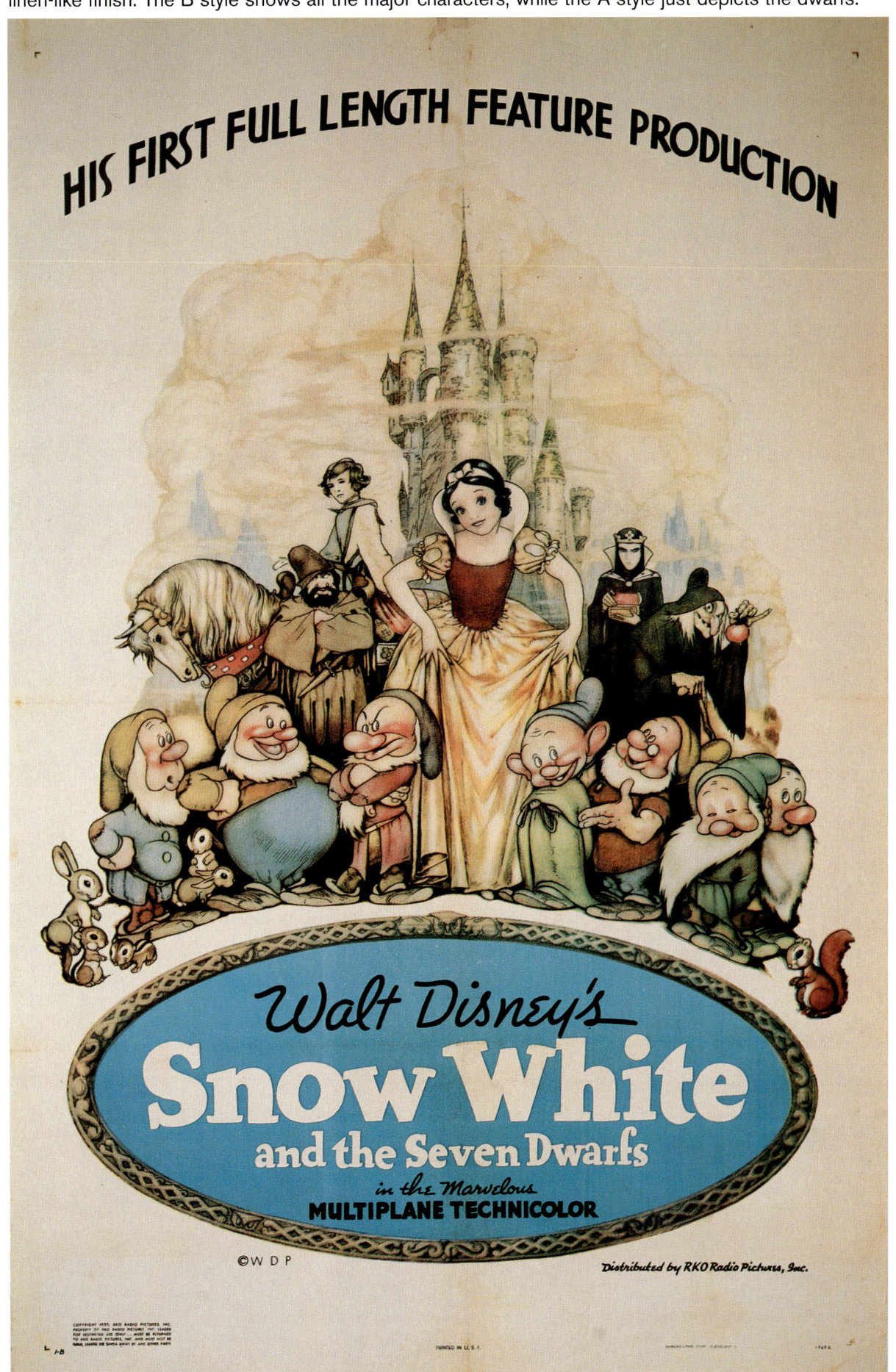

27. Snow White and the Seven Dwarfs, Walt Disney, 1937, style B one-sheet, Cond. B, linenbacked, 41 x 27 in $10,000-15,000

Most half-sheets were folded twice to make for easy mailing, but the one offered here is unfolded. Also offered is a rare silk banner with its original attachments for displaying it in theaters.

28. Snow White and the Seven Dwarfs, Walt Disney, 1937, half-sheet, Cond. B+, unfolded, 22 x 28 in $5,000-7,000

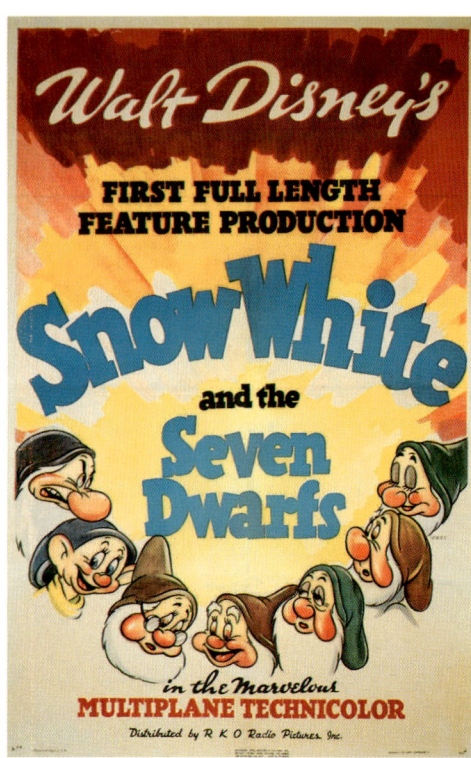

29. Snow White and the Seven Dwarfs, Walt Disney, 1937, style A one-sheet, Cond. B-, linen-backed, 41 x 27 in $1,000-1,500

30. Snow White and the Seven Dwarfs, Walt Disney, 1937, silk banner, Cond. A-, 50 x 37 in $1,000-1,500

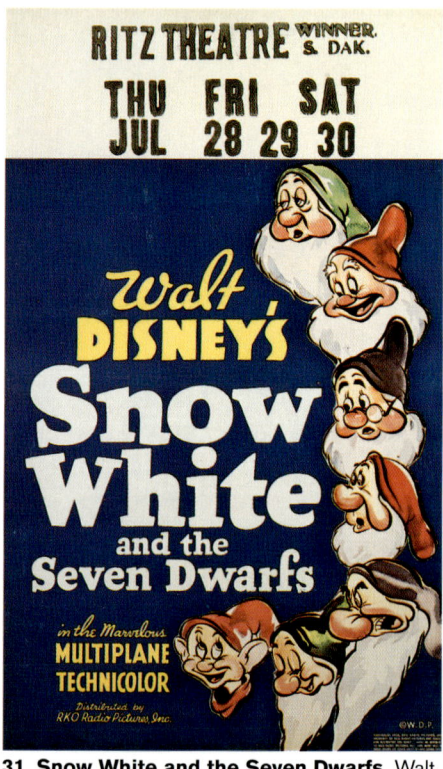

31. Snow White and the Seven Dwarfs, Walt Disney, 1938, window card, Cond. A-, 22 x 14 in $600-800

Each of the lobby cards offered here depicts a key scene from the film. The set of eight lobby cards is in immaculate condition. Also offered is a never before seen set of eight deluxe color stills.

32. Snow White and the Seven Dwarfs, Walt Disney, 1937, set of eight lobby cards (six pictured), Cond. A, each 11 x 14 in $5,000-7,000

33. Snow White and the Seven Dwarfs, Walt Disney, 1937, set of eight DeLuxe Photos (Color-Glos) (two pictured), Cond. B-, each 11 x 14 in $400-600

Sporting events are natural subjects for film, both for the inherent action of the sport and the name recognition of the real-life sports figures, who often had leading roles in these films.

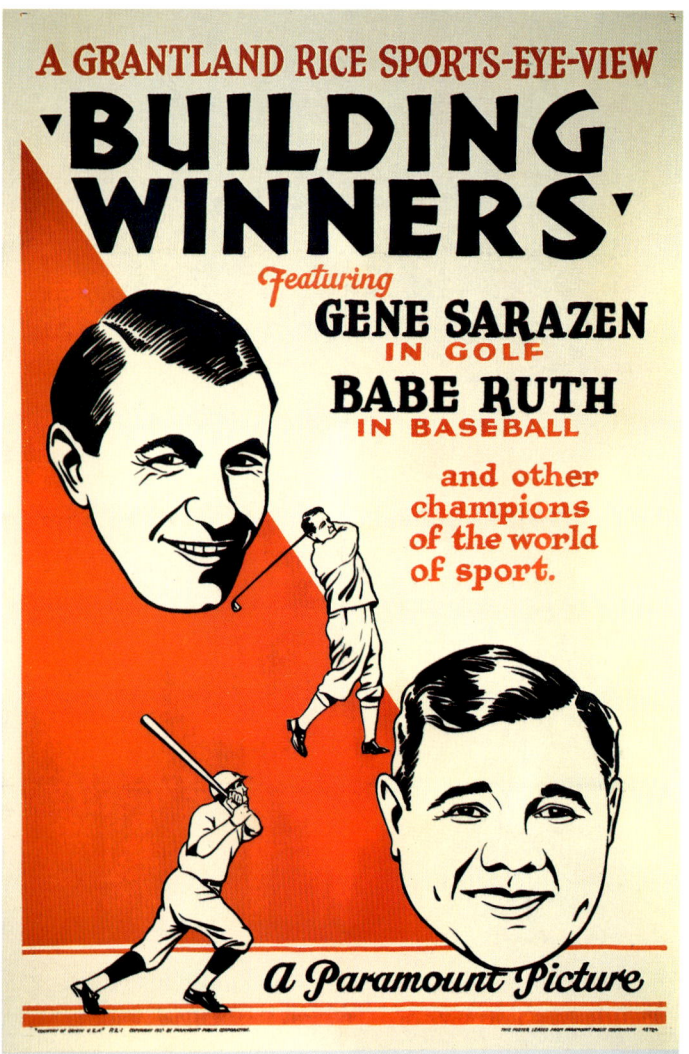

34. Building Winners, Paramount, 1932, one-sheet, Cond. B, linenbacked, 41 x 27 in $2,000-3,000

35. Love in the Rough, MGM, 1930, one-sheet, Cond. A-, 41 x 27 in $1,000-1,500

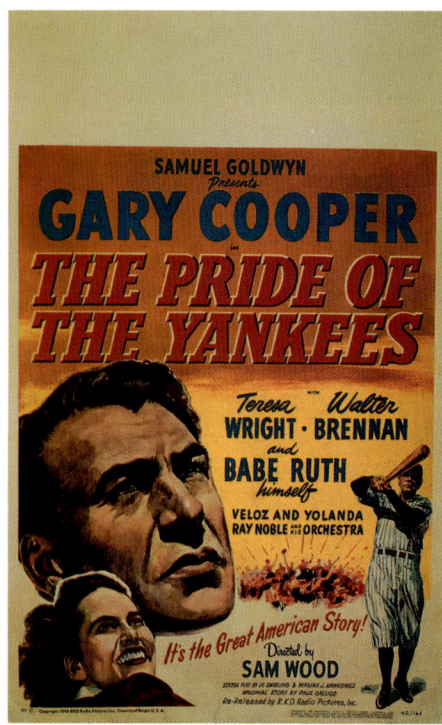

36. The Pride of the Yankees, RKO, 1949 reissue, window card, Cond. B, paperbacked, 22 x 14 in $300-500

37. Casey at the Mets, Universal, 1963, one-sheet, Cond. A-, 41 x 27 in $400-600

38. Out of Bounds, Paramount, circa 1931, one-sheet, Cond. B-, linenbacked, 41 x 27 in $600-800

In the days before television, almost every major fight was filmed and released to theaters. A group of six one-sheets from famous matches is offered.

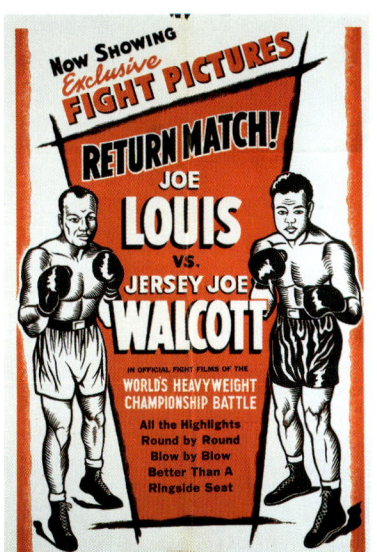
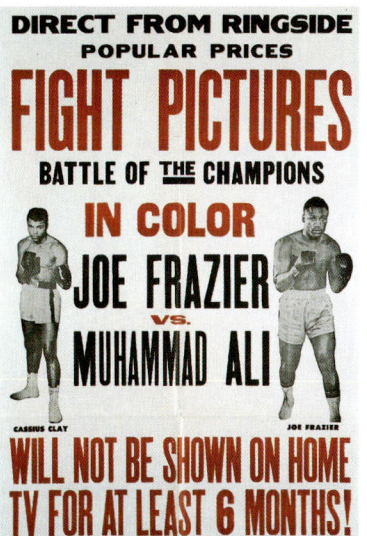

39. 6 Boxing Posters, six one-sheets (two pictured), list on request, Cond. A- to B+, each 41 x 27 in $1,000-1,500

40. Wolgast-Nelson Fight Pictures, circa 1908, one-sheet, Cond. B, linenbacked, 41 x 27 in $600-800

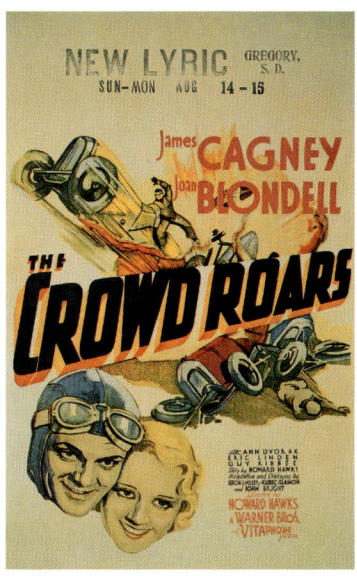

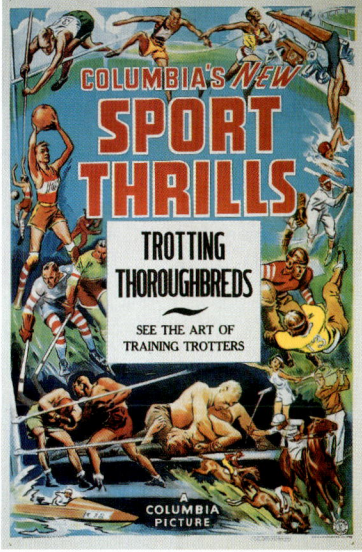

41. The Crowd Roars, Warner Brothers, 1932, window card, Cond. B, paperbacked, 22 x 14 in $500-700

42. High Speed, Columbia, 1932, window card, Cond. B+, 22 x 14 in $200-400

43. Trotting Thoroughbreds, Columbia, 1937, one-sheet, Cond. B+, linenbacked, 41 x 27 in $400-600

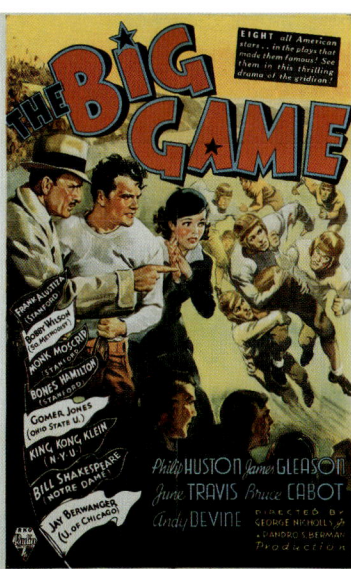

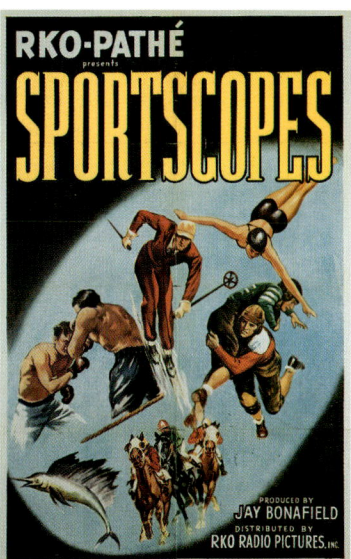

44. The Big Game, RKO, 1936, one-sheet, Cond. A-, 41 x 27 in $400-600

45. Touchdown, Paramount, 1931, window card, Cond. B+, 22 x 14 in $200-400

46. Sportscopes, RKO, 1947, one-sheet, Cond. B+, 41 x 27 in $400-600

The Valiant was Paul Muni's very first film. **Seed** was one of Bette Davis' earliest efforts. Barbara Stanwyck performed in a series of racy films (most for Columbia Studios) in the early 1930s.

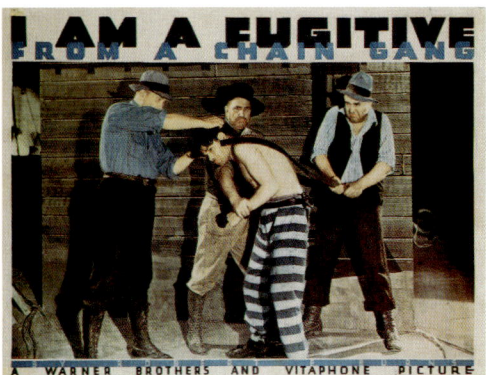

47. I am a Fugitive From a Chain Gang, Warner Brothers, 1932, lobby card, Cond. B, 11 x 14 in
$500-700

48. A Tale of Two Cities, MGM, 1935, set of eight lobby cards (one pictured), Cond. B+, each 11 x 14 in
$700-900

49. The Valiant, William Fox, 1929, three lobby cards (one pictured), Cond. B+, each 11 x 14 in $500-700

50. Seed, Universal, 1931, set of eight lobby cards (one pictured), Cond. A- to B+, each 11 x 14 in $400-600

51. Forbidden, Columbia, 1932, five lobby cards (one pictured), Cond. A- to B+, each 11 x 14 in $600-800

52. Shopworn, Columbia, 1932, three lobby cards (one pictured), Cond. A, each 11 x 14 in $300-500

53. Night Nurse, Warner Brothers, 1931, two lobby cards (one pictured), Cond. A-, each 11 x 14 in
$200-400

54. Ten Cents a Dance, Columbia, 1931, lobby card, Cond. A, 11 x 14 in $100-200

Swashbuckler films have always been extremely popular, and the greatest star of these films was Errol Flynn. Most film buffs agree that **The Adventures of Robin Hood** was his finest film.

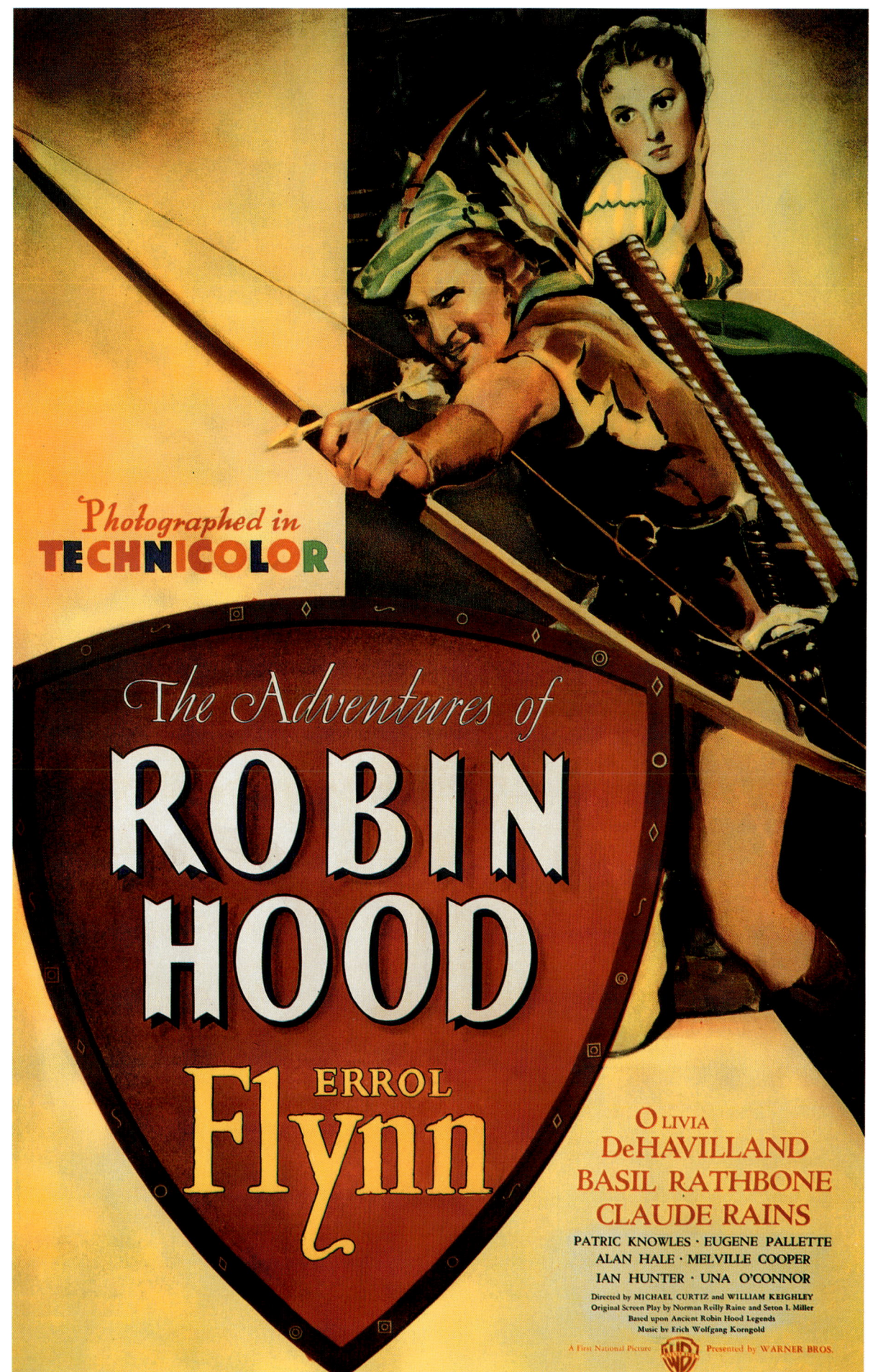

55. The Adventures of Robin Hood, Warner Brothers, 1938, one-sheet, Cond. B, linenbacked, 41 x 27 in $9,000-12,000

John Barrymore made some of his greatest films in the early 1930s. One of these, **A Bill of Divorcement,** was also Katherine Hepburn's film debut.

56. Blonde Crazy, Warner Brothers, 1931, four lobby cards (one pictured), Cond. A- to B+, each 11 x 14 in $1,500-2,000

57. It Happened One Night, Columbia, 1934, lobby card, Cond. B, 11 x 14 in $700-900

58. Counsellor-At-Law, Universal, 1933, set of eight lobby cards (one pictured), Cond. A to A-, each 11 x 14 in $800-1,000

59. Arsene Lupin, MGM, 1932, three lobby cards (one pictured), Cond. A, each 11 x 14 in $500-700

60. A Bill of Divorcement, RKO, 1932, window card, Cond. B-, 22 x 14 in $700-900

61. Thin Ice, 20th Century Fox, 1937, one-sheet, Cond. B+, linenbacked, 41 x 27 in $600-800

62. Cafe Metropole, TC Fox, 1937, one-sheet, Cond. B+, linenbacked, 41 x 27 in $600-800

Film noir is one of the most collected genres, and the most desired film noir poster is **This Gun For Hire**, which many consider one of the finest film posters ever created.

63. This Gun For Hire, Paramount, 1942, one-sheet, Cond. B+, linenbacked, 41 x 27 in
$5,000-7,000

64. The Blue Dahlia, Paramount, 1946, one-sheet, Cond. B+, linenbacked, 41 x 27 in
$2,000-3,000

65. The Glass Key, Paramount, 1942, one-sheet, Cond. B, linenbacked, 41 x 27 in
$1,500-2,000

66. Calcutta, Paramount, 1947, one-sheet, Cond. B+, linenbacked, 41 x 27 in $700-900

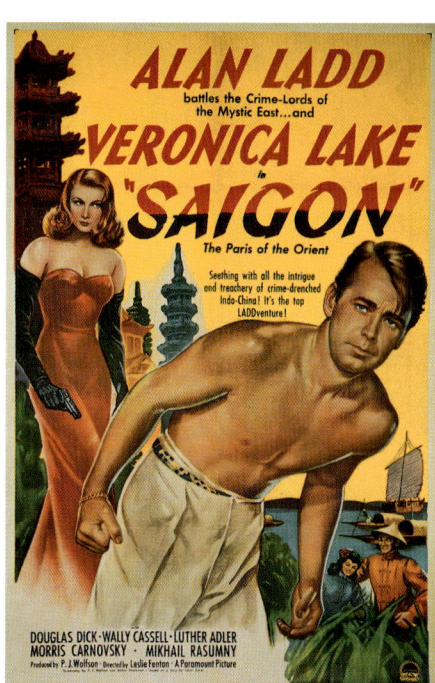

67. Saigon, Paramount, 1948, one-sheet, Cond. B+, linenbacked, 41 x 27 in $700-900

This Gun For Hire and **Out of the Past** were given early reissues with new and different posters. The reissue posters are much harder to find than the originals.

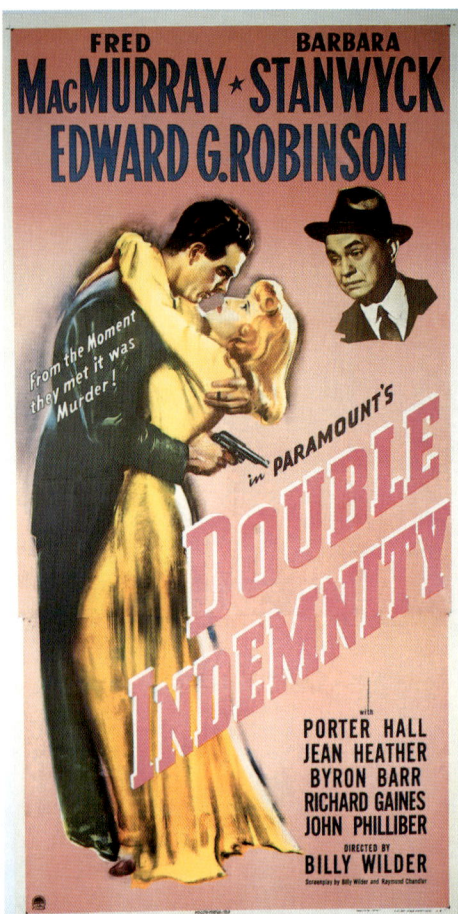

68. Double Indemnity, Paramount, 1944, three-sheet, Cond. B+, linenbacked, 81 x 41 in
$1,000-1,500

69. Thank You, Mr. Moto, 20th Century Fox, 1937, three-sheet, Cond. B, linenbacked, 81 x 41 in
$900-1,200

70. Where Danger Lives, RKO, 1950, three-sheet, Cond. B+, linenbacked, 81 x 41 in
$900-1,200

71. The Blue Dahlia, Paramount, 1946, insert, Cond. B, 36 x 14 in
$700-900

72. This Gun For Hire, Paramount, 1945 reissue, insert, Cond. B, 36 x 14 in
$600-800

73. Out of the Past, RKO, 1953 reissue, insert, Cond. B+, 36 x 14 in
$300-500

74. The Brasher Doubloon, 20th Century Fox, 1946, insert, Cond. B+, 36 x 14 in $200-400

Perhaps World War II and its aftermath contributed to the popularity of film noir, as the 1940s saw a considerable number of these films, some made by top stars and directors.

75. Leave Her to Heaven, 20th Century Fox, 1945, one-sheet, Cond. B+, 41 x 27 in $800-1,000

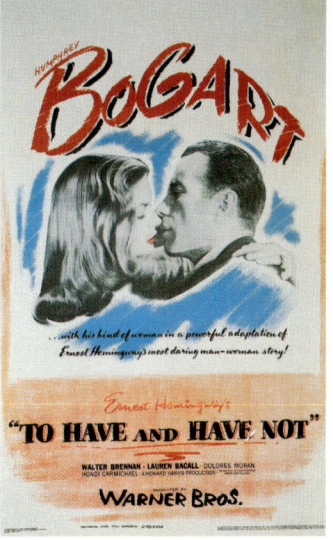

76. To Have and Have Not, Warner Brothers, 1944, one-sheet, Cond. B, linenbacked, 41 x 27 in $600-800

77. The Big Shot, Warner Brothers, 1942, window card, Cond. B, paper-backed, 22 x 14 in $200-300

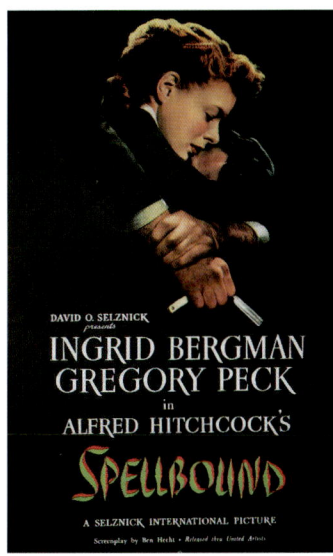

78. Spellbound, United Artists, 1945, one-sheet, Cond. B-, linen-backed, 41 x 27 in $900-1,200

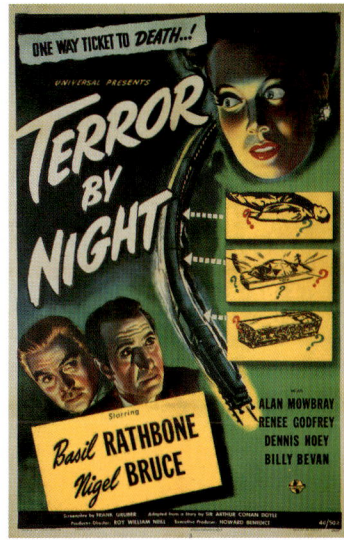

79. Terror By Night, Universal, 1945, one-sheet, Cond. B, linenbacked, 41 x 27 in $500-700

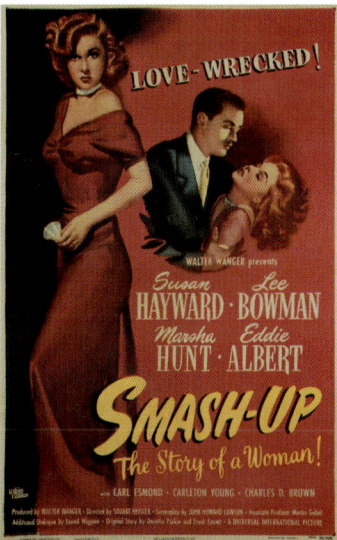

80. Smash-Up, Universal, 1946, one-sheet, Cond. B, linenbacked, 41 x 27 in $500-700

81. Sorry, Wrong Number, Paramount, 1948, one-sheet, Cond. B+, linenbacked, 41 x 27 in $500-700

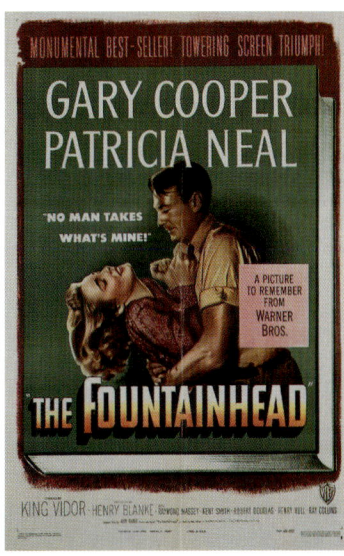

82. The Fountainhead, Warner Brothers, 1949, one-sheet, Cond. B+, 41 x 27 in $600-800

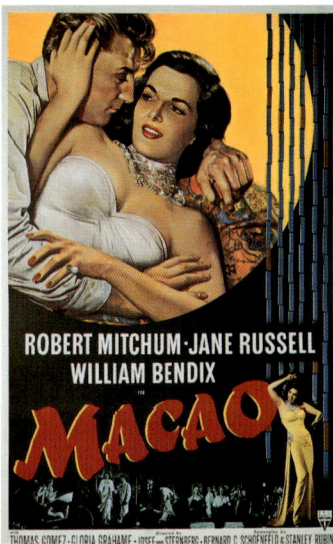

83. Macao, RKO, 1952, one-sheet, Cond. B+, linenbacked, 41 x 27 in $500-700

There were many popular detective series of films, but none was more popular in the 1930s than Charlie Chan, most noteably portrayed by Swedish actor Warner Oland.

84. Charlie Chan at the Race Track, 20th Century Fox, 1936, one-sheet, Cond. B+, linenbacked, 41 x 27 in $4,000-6,000

85. Raffles, United Artists, 1939, one-sheet, Cond. B, linenbacked, 41 x 27 in $800-1,000

86. Phantoms, Inc., MGM, 1945, one-sheet, Cond. B+, 41 x 27 in $400-600

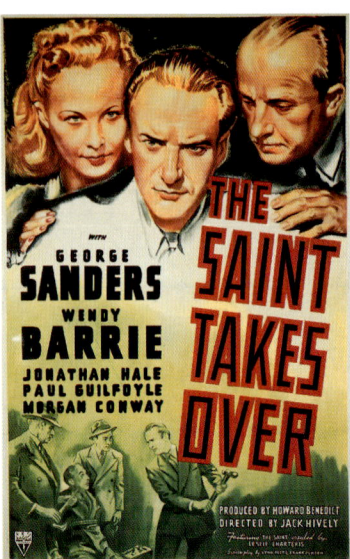

87. The Saint Takes Over, RKO, 1940, one-sheet, Cond. B, linenbacked, 41 x 27 in $600-800

88. The Falcon Takes Over, RKO, 1942, one-sheet, Cond. B, linenbacked, 41 x 27 in $500-700

89. Some Blondes are Dangerous, Universal, 1937, one-sheet, Cond. B+, linenbacked, 41 x 27 in $400-600

Lobby cards from some of the best film noir are offered here. The Title card from **Gun Crazy** was signed by the film's director, Joseph Lewis.

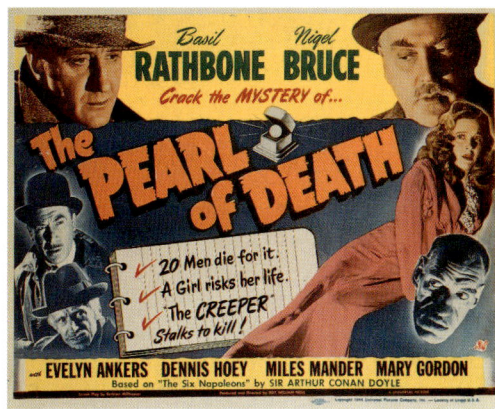

91. 14 Sherlock Holmes lobby cards, Universal, 1942-46, list on request, 14 lobby cards (one pictured), Cond. A- to B, each 11 x 14 in $700-900

90. 10 Bogart lobby cards, 1940s and 1950s, list on request, 10 lobby cards (two pictured), Cond. B+ to C+, each 11 x 14 in $600-800

92. Gun Crazy, United Artists, 1950, Title card, signed by Joseph Lewis, Cond. A-, 11 x 14 in $400-600

93. The Blue Dahlia, Paramount, 1946, seven lobby cards (one pictured), Cond. A- to B, each 11 x 14 in $600-800

94. Murder, My Sweet, RKO, 1944, half-sheet, Cond. B+, 22 x 28 in $400-600

95. 7 Charlie Chan lobby cards, Fox and Monogram, 1930s and 1940s, list on request, 7 lobby cards (one pictured), Cond. A- to B+, each 11 x 14 in $200-400

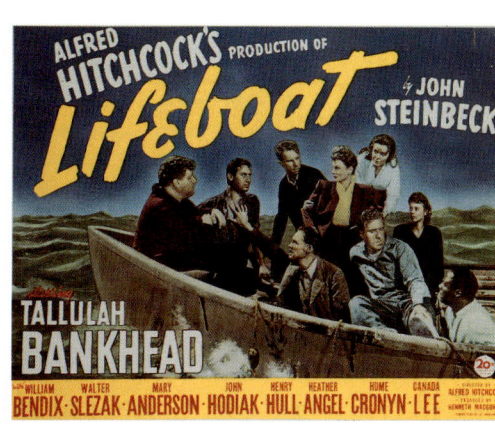

96. Lifeboat, 20th Century Fox, 1943, Title card, Cond. A, 11 x 14 in $200-400

This auction contains an amazing find of short subject posters from the early 1930s that was recently discovered. Many have never been seen before, and most are in excellent condition.

97. Washington, the Man and the Capitol, Vitaphone, circa 1932, one-sheet, Cond. B+, 41 x 27 in $500-700

98. The Prisoner of Swing, Vitaphone, 1938, one-sheet, Cond. A-, 41 x 27 in $500-700

99. Broadway Ballyhoo, Vitaphone, 1935, one-sheet, Cond. A-, 41 x 27 in $500-700

100. Pepper Pot Novelty, Vitaphone, circa 1933, one-sheet, Cond. B, linen-backed, 41 x 27 in $400-600

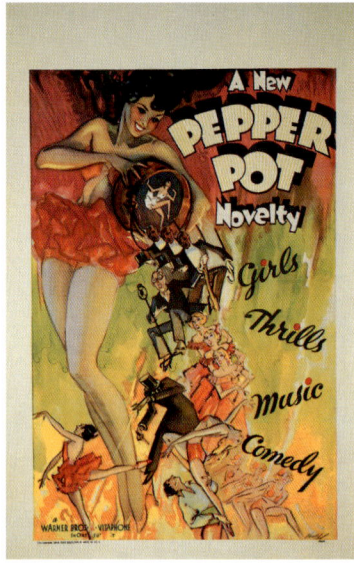

101. A New Pepper Pot Novelty, Warner Brothers, circa 1935, one-sheet, Cond. B+, linenbacked, 41 x 27 in $400-600

102. Melody Master Bands, Vitaphone, 1936, one-sheet, Cond. B, linenbacked, 41 x 27 in $400-600

103. Double or Nothing, Vitaphone, 1936, one-sheet, Cond. B+, 41 x 27 in $400-600

104. Broadway Brevities, Vitaphone, circa 1935, one-sheet, Cond. B, 41 x 27 in $400-600

105. Vaudeville Show, Vitaphone, circa 1934, one-sheet, Cond. B, 41 x 27 in $400-600

The Jazz Singer is one of the great landmarks of film. It is widely remembered as the first "talkie". Its success marked the end of silent film and the birth of the movie musical. Posters from this film are extremely rare. One of the two known copies of the one-sheet is offered.

106. The Jazz Singer, Warner Brothers, 1927, one-sheet, Cond. B, linenbacked, 41 x 27 in $15,000-$20,000

Fred Astaire and Ginger Rogers created a series of musical films in the 1930s that have never been equalled. Posters from some of the best of these are offered.

107. Swing Time, RKO, 1936, one-sheet, Cond. B+, linenbacked, 41 x 27 in
$3,000-5,000

108. Shall We Dance, RKO, 1937, one-sheet, Cond. B, linenbacked, 41 x 27 in
$3,000-5,000

109. Carefree, RKO, 1938, one-sheet, Cond. C+, linenbacked, 41 x 27 in $2,000-4,000

110. The Story of Vernon and Irene Castle, RKO, 1939, one-sheet, Cond. B-, linenbacked, 41 x 27 in $1,000-1,500

111. A Damsel in Distress, RKO, 1937, one-sheet, Cond. B, linenbacked, 41 x 27 in
$900-1,200

Light-hearted musicals were very popular in the early 1940s. Perhaps this was because they allowed the viewer to escape the harsh realities of World War II.

112. Pigskin Parade, 20th Century Fox, 1936, one-sheet, Cond. B, linen-backed, 41 x 27 in $400-600

113. Babes in Arms, MGM, 1939, one-sheet, Cond. B, linenbacked, 41 x 27 in $500-700

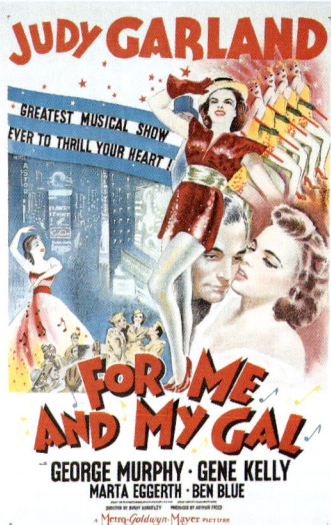

114. For Me and My Gal, MGM, 1942, one-sheet, Cond. B, linen-backed, 41 x 27 in $600-800

115. Presenting Lily Mars, MGM, 1943, one-sheet, Cond. B, linen-backed, 41 x 27 in $500-700

116. A Star is Born, Warner Brothers, 1954, one-sheet, Cond. B+, linenbacked, 41 x 27 in $400-600

117. Footlight Serenade, 20th Century Fox, 1942, one-sheet, Cond. B+, linenbacked, 41 x 27 in $500-700

118. Road to Singapore, Paramount, 1940, one-sheet, Cond. B+, 41 x 27 in $500-700

119. Holiday Inn, Paramount, 1942, one-sheet, Cond. B+, 41 x 27 in $300-500

120. Hello, Frisco, Hello, 20th Century Fox, 1943, one-sheet, Cond. B, linenbacked, 41 x 27 in $500-700

Musicals remained popular throughout the 1950s, and two of the finest were **An American in Paris**, which won the Best Picture Oscar, and **Singin' in the Rain**.

121. 100 Men and a Girl, Universal, 1937, one-sheet, Cond. B+, linen-backed, 41 x 27 in $600-800

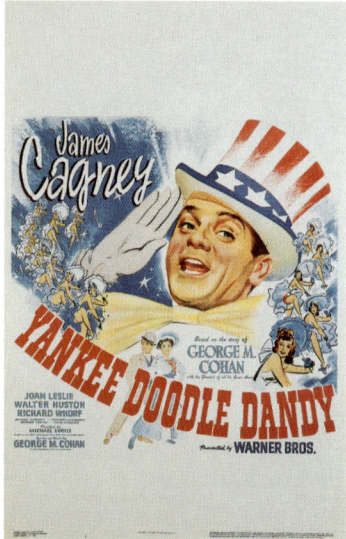

122. Yankee Doodle Dandy, Warner Brothers, 1942, window card, Cond. A, 22 x 14 in $300-500

123. An American in Paris, MGM, 1951, one-sheet, Cond. B+, linen-backed, 41 x 27 in $500-700

124. Singin' in the Rain, MGM, 1952, window card, Cond. B+, 22 x 14 in $200-400

125. Easter Parade, MGM, 1948, style C one-sheet, Cond. B+, linen-backed, 41 x 27 in $600-800

126. Easter Parade, MGM, 1948, style D one-sheet, Cond. B, linen-backed, 41 x 27 in $500-700

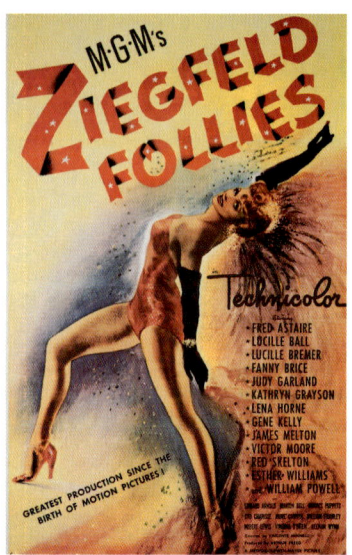

127. Ziegfeld Follies, MGM, 1945, one-sheet, Cond. B-, linenbacked, 41 x 27 in $900-1,200

128. Ziegfeld Girl, MGM, 1941, one-sheet, Cond. B, linenbacked, 41 x 27 in $600-800

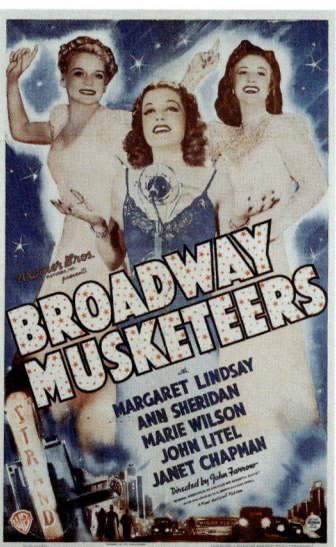

129. Broadway Musketeers, Warner Brothers, 1938, one-sheet, Cond. B+, 41 x 27 in $400-600

Veronica Lake was extremely popular in the early 1940s. Noted illustrator McClelland Barclay was hired to create the one-sheet for **I Wanted Wings**.

130. I Wanted Wings, Paramount, 1941, one-sheet, Cond. B+, linenbacked, 41 x 27 in $700-900

131. I Married A Witch, Paramount, 1942, one-sheet, Cond. B+, linenbacked, 41 x 27 in $700-900

132. One of Our Aircraft Is Missing, United Artists, 1942, one-sheet, Cond. B+, linenbacked, 41 x 27 in $600-800

133. Going My Way, Paramount, 1944, one-sheet, Cond. B, 41 x 27 in $300-500

134. The Bells of St. Mary's, RKO, 1945, one-sheet, Cond. B+, 41 x 27 in $300-500

Movie poster artists loved to put a beautiful star on a poster, often using their talents to enhance the star's appearance to make her even more glamourous.

135. The Women, MGM, 1939, one-sheet, Cond. A-, 41 x 27 in $900-1,200

136. Jezebel, Warner Brothers, 1938, "other company" one-sheet, Cond. B, linenbacked, 41 x 27 in $1,000-1,500

137. Hearts Divided, Warner Brothers, 1936, one-sheet, Cond. B+, linenbacked, 41 x 27 in $400-600

138. The Bride Walks Out, RKO, 1936, one-sheet, Cond. B, linenbacked, 41 x 27 in $400-600

139. Three on a Match, Warner Brothers, 1932, window card, Cond. B-, half-inch border trim, 22 x 13 in $500-700

Virtually no billboard size posters survive from pre-1940 films, for they were normally glued to walls and not taken down. A happy exception is this twenty-four-sheet from **Jezebel.**

140. Jezebel, Warner Brothers, 1938, twenty-four-sheet, Cond. B, linenbacked, 9 x 20 ft

$7,000-10,000

141. Our Teddy, First National, 1919, one-sheet, Cond. B, linenbacked, 41 x 27 in

$1,000-1,500

142. Believe It or Not, Vitaphone, 1931, one-sheet, Cond. B+, linenbacked, 41 x 27 in

$1,000-1,500

In the 1930s, theatergoers saw two features, as well as a short subject, a cartoon, and a newsreel. Posters were made for all of these, but few survive from non-feature films.

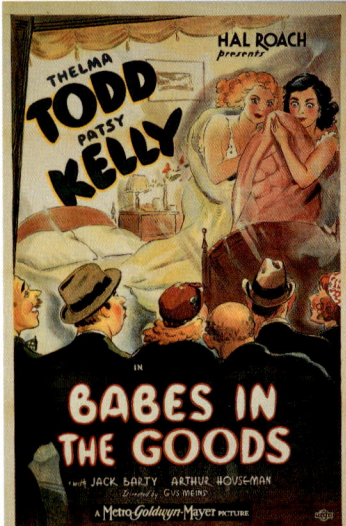

143. Babes in the Goods, MGM, 1934, one-sheet, Cond. B+, linen-backed, 41 x 27 in $500-700

144. Mixed Nuts, MGM, 1933, one-sheet, Cond. B, linenbacked, 41 x 27 in $500-700

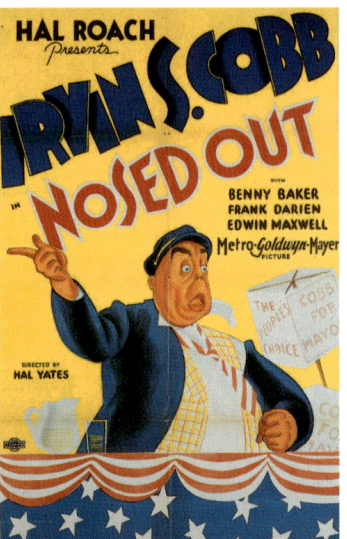

145. Nosed Out, MGM, 1934, one-sheet, Cond. A-, 41 x 27 in $500-700

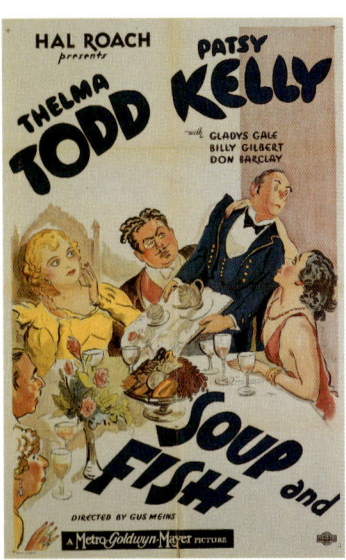

146. Soup and Fish, MGM, 1934, one-sheet, Cond. B+, 41 x 27 in $500-700

147. Casa Manana Revue, MGM, 1938, one-sheet, Cond. B+, 41 x 27 in $500-700

148. Captain Kidd's Treasure, MGM, 1938, one-sheet, Cond. A-, 41 x 27 in $500-700

149. What Do You Think, MGM, 1937, one-sheet, Cond. B+, 41 x 27 in $500-700

150. That's Why I Left You, MGM, 1943, one-sheet, Cond. B-, linenbacked, 41 x 27 in $500-700

151. Nostradamus, MGM, 1938, one-sheet, Cond. B, 41 x 27 in $500-700

Krazy Kat was one of the most popular newspaper comic strips, and the character appeared in many silent and sound cartoons, but few posters from any of them are known to have survived.

152. Krazy Spooks, Columbia, 1933, one-sheet, Cond. B, linenbacked, 41 x 27 in $6,000-8,000

Cartoons in the early 1930s were dominated by Walt Disney and the Fleischer brothers. The other studios made cartoons as well, but none achieved the same level of success.

153. The Explorer, Educational, 1931, one-sheet, Cond. B, linenbacked, 41 x 27 in $1,000-1,500

154. Cubby Bear, RKO, 1933, one-sheet, Cond. A-, 41 x 27 in
$1,000-1,500

155. Circus Days, Fox, 1935, one-sheet, Cond. B, linenbacked, 41 x 27 in $600-800

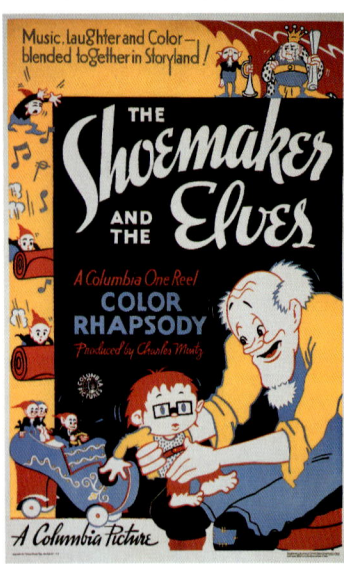

156. The Shoemaker and the Elves, Columbia, 1934, one-sheet, Cond. B, linenbacked, 41 x 27 in
$900-1,200

157. Playing Politics, Columbia, 1936, one-sheet, Cond. B, linenbacked, 41 x 27 in $700-900

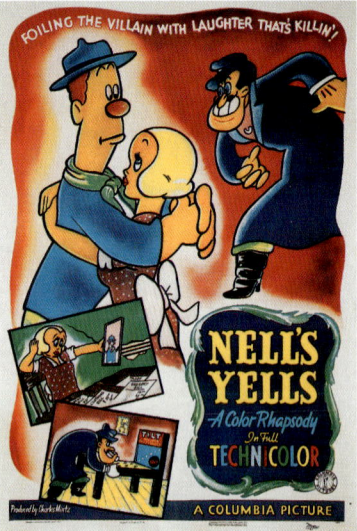

158. Nell's Yells, Columbia, 1939, one-sheet, Cond. B, linenbacked, 41 x 27 in $600-800

159. Scrap for Victory, 20th Century Fox, 1943, one-sheet, Cond. B, 41 x 27 in $600-800

160. Bosko and the Pirates, MGM, 1937, one-sheet, Cond. A-, 41 x 27 in
$600-800

161. Tom and Jerry, MGM, circa 1948, Spanish one-sheet, Cond. B+, 41 x 27 in $500-700

One of the best-remembered cartoon characters of the 1930s was Betty Boop, but sadly few posters are known, especially those from the more daring pre-Hayes code era.

162. I Heard, Paramount, 1933, one-sheet, Cond. B, linenbacked, 41 x 27 in — $7,000-9,000

163. Another New Paramount Talkartoon, Paramount, circa 1932, one-sheet, Cond. B, linenbacked, 41 x 27 in $6,000-8,000

164. Romantic Melodies, Paramount, 1932, one-sheet, Cond. A-, 41 x 27 in $4,000-6,000

165. Making Friends, Paramount, 1936, one-sheet, Cond. B+, 41 x 27 in $3,000-5,000

166. Be Human, Paramount, 1936, one-sheet, Cond. B, 41 x 27 in $3,000-5,000

Before Betty Boop received her own series, she appeared in a series of films known as **Paramount Talkartoons**, often appearing with Koko the Clown.

After the huge success of Betty Boop, the Fleischers introduced Popeye in 1934, who also achieved huge success. Two extremely early Popeye posters are offered.

167. Sock-a-Bye, Baby, Paramount, 1934, one-sheet, Cond. B+, linenbacked, 41 x 27 in $4,000-6,000

168. Another New Popeye Comedy, Paramount, 1934, one-sheet, Cond. B+, linenbacked, 41 x 27 in $2,000-3,000

169. Let's All Sing Like the Birdies Sing, Paramount, 1934, one-sheet, Cond. B, linenbacked, 41 x 27 in $900-1,200

170. Paramount Screen Song, Paramount, circa 1932, one-sheet, Cond. B, linenbacked, 41 x 27 in $800-1,000

171. Mr. Bug Goes To Town, Paramount, 1941, one-sheet, Cond. B, 41 x 27 in $400-600

Warner Brothers had its greatest cartoon success in the middle 1930s, as it introduced the characters who quickly became household names.

172. A New Looney Tune, Vitaphone, circa 1934, one-sheet, Cond. A-, 41 x 27 in $1,500-2,000

173. Merrie Melodies, Vitaphone, circa 1934, one-sheet, Cond. B+, 41 x 27 in $1,000-1,500

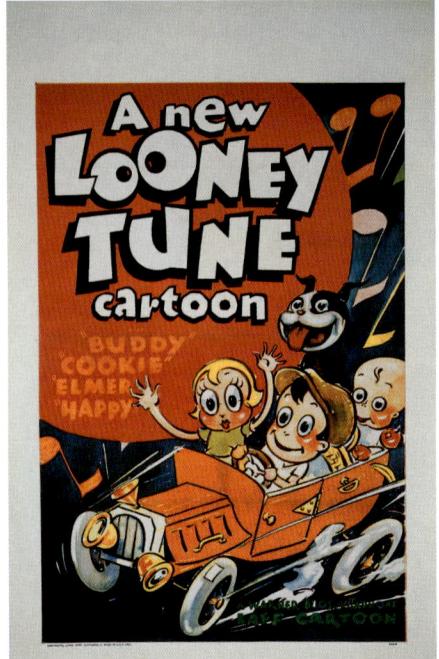

174. A New Looney Tune Cartoon, Warner Bros./Vitaphone, circa 1935, one-sheet, Cond. B, linenbacked, 41 x 27 in $1,000-1,500

175. The Merrie Melodies, Vitaphone, circa 1932, one-sheet, Cond. B+, 41 x 27 in $900-1,200

176. A Warner Bros. Cartoon, Warner Brothers, 1948, one-sheet, Cond. B+, 41 x 27 in $700-900

Studios kept releasing new cartoon characters, hoping to match the success of Mickey Mouse. Many of these were short-lived, and their posters are very rare.

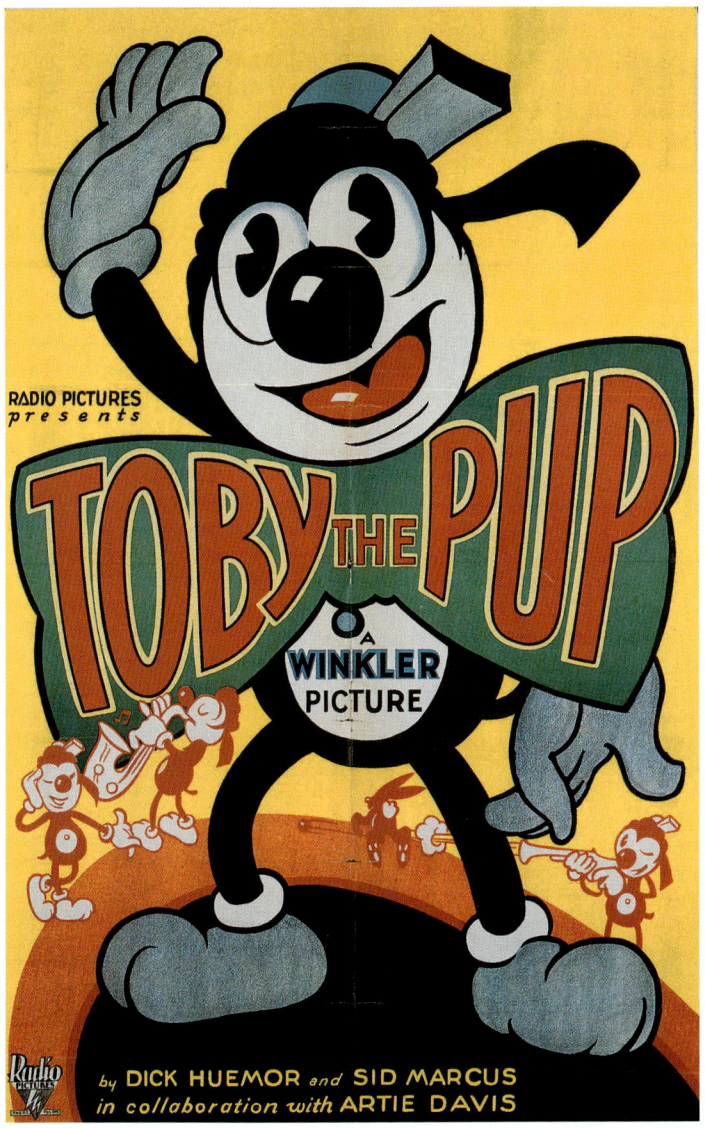

177. Toby the Pup, RKO, 1930, one-sheet, Cond. B, 41 x 27 in
$1,000-1,500

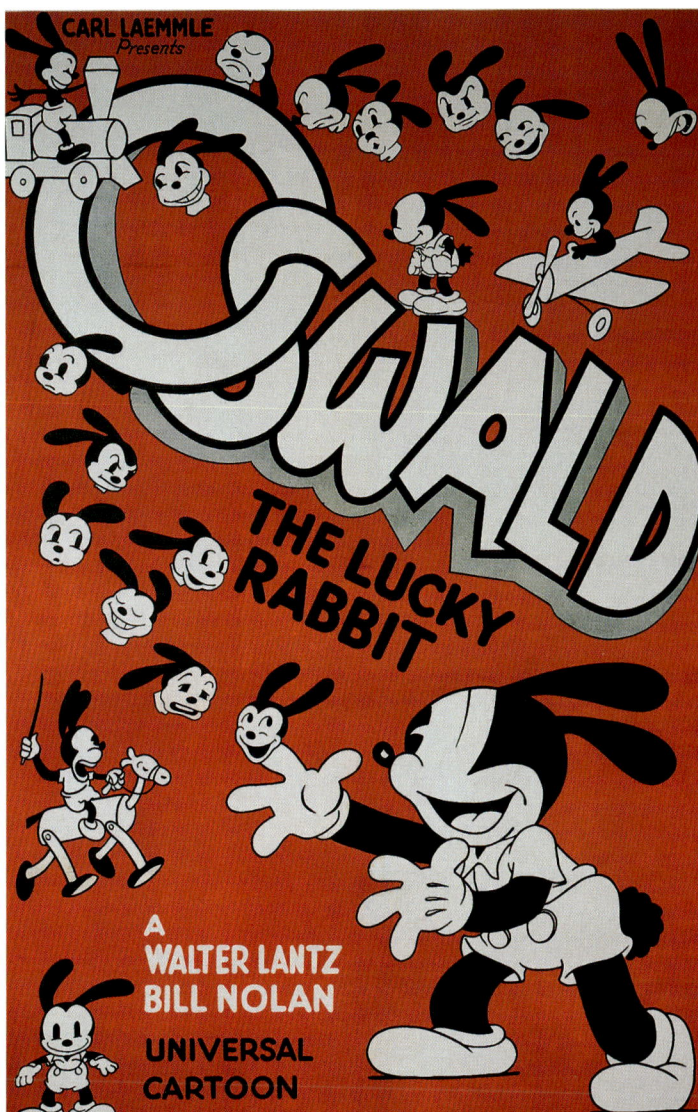

178. Oswald the Lucky Rabbit, Universal, circa 1935, one-sheet, Cond. B+, 41 x 27 in
$1,000-1,500

179. Oswald the Lucky Rabbit, Universal, 1935, one-sheet, Cond. B+, linenbacked, 41 x 27 in
$1,000-1,500

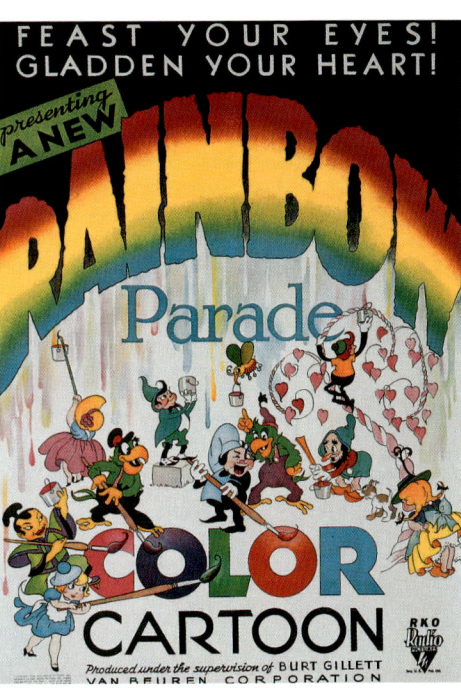

180. Rainbow Parade, RKO, 1934, one-sheet, Cond. B, linenbacked, 41 x 27 in
$1,000-1,500

181. Rainbow Parade, RKO, 1935, one-sheet, Cond. B, linenbacked, 41 x 27 in
$900-1,200

The studios would often put new actors and directors to work in their short subjects. Betty Grable made one of her earliest appearances in **School For Romance.**

182. Magic Carpet of Movietone, Fox, circa 1933, one-sheet, Cond. B-, 41 x 27 in $500-700

183. Adventures of the News Reel Cameraman, Fox, circa 1933, one-sheet, Cond. B, 41 x 27 in $400-600

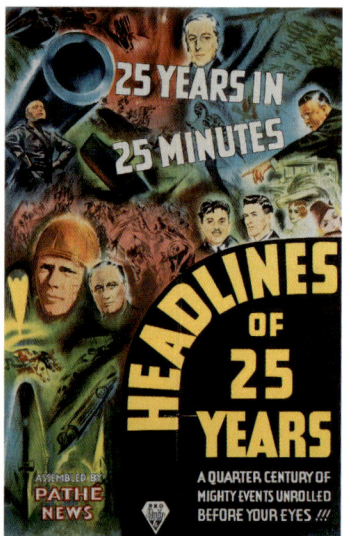

184. Headlines of 25 Years, RKO, 1936, one-sheet, Cond. B+, 41 x 27 in $400-600

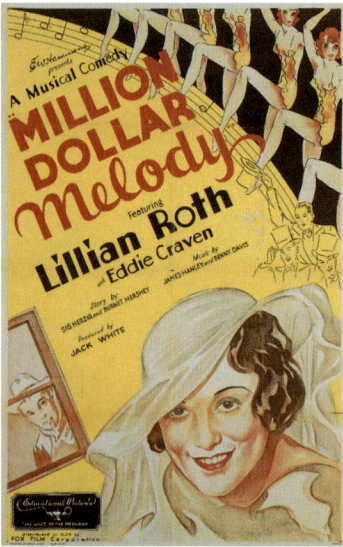

185. Million Dollar Melody, Fox, 1933, one-sheet, Cond. B, 41 x 27 in $500-700

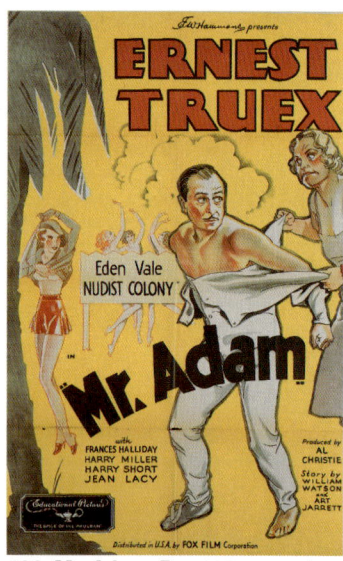

186. Mr. Adam, Fox, 1934, one-sheet, Cond. B+, 41 x 27 in $500-700

187. Gags and Gals, 20th Century Fox, 1936, one-sheet, Cond. B, linenbacked, 41 x 27 in $500-700

188. School For Romance, Columbia, 1934, one-sheet, Cond. B+, 41 x 27 in $500-700

189. Court of Human Relations, Columbia, 1936, one-sheet, Cond. A-, 41 x 27 in $400-600

190. On the Air and Off, Universal, 1933, one-sheet, Cond. B+, linenbacked, 41 x 27 in $400-600

Lon Chaney was the first great horror star and **The Phantom of the Opera** was his most memorable role. Universal dominated horror films throughout the 1920s, 1930s, and 1940s.

191. The Phantom of the Opera, Universal, 1925, Title card, Cond. B+, 11 x 14 in $2,000-3,000

192. Frankenstein Meets the Wolf Man, Universal, 1943, Title card, Cond. B, 11 x 14 in $800-1,000

193. The House of Frankenstein, Universal, 1944, Title card, Cond. B, 11 x 14 in $700-900

194. The Mummy's Curse, Universal, 1944, lobby card, Cond. B+, 11 x 14 in $200-400

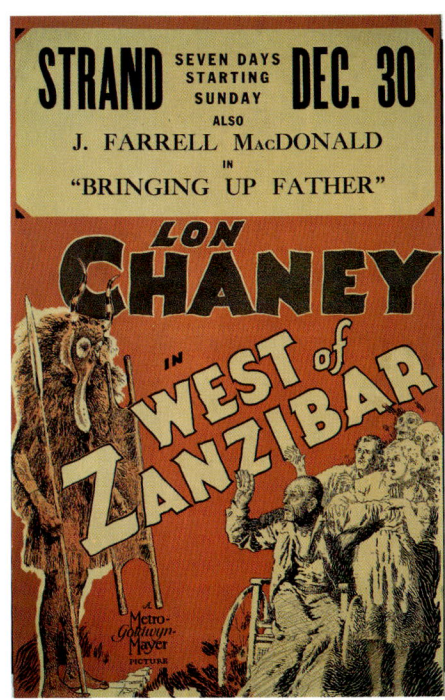

195. West of Zanzibar, MGM, 1928, window card, Cond. B, paperbacked, 22 x 14 in $300-500

196. Them, Warner Brothers, 1954, one-sheet, Cond. B+, 41 x 27 in $400-600

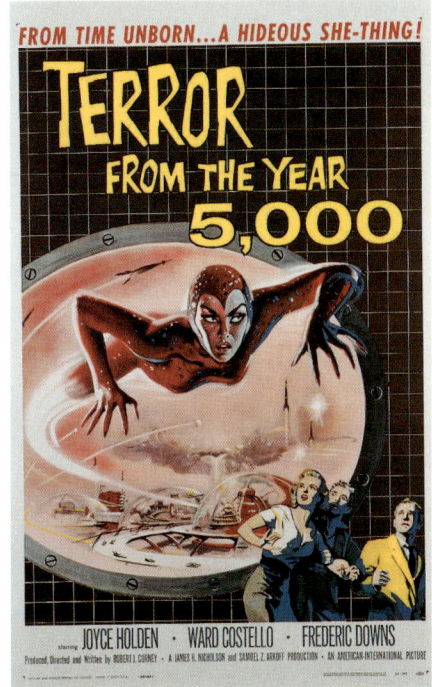

197. Terror From the Year 5,000, A.I.P., 1958, one-sheet, Cond. A-, 41 x 27 in $500-700

One of the only major film monsters that was created after 1945 was the **Creature From the Black Lagoon**. An extremely rare six-sheet is offered.

198. Flight to Mars, Monogram, 1951, half-sheet, Cond. B+, 22 x 28 in $200-400

199. Target Earth, Allied Artists, 1954, half-sheet, Cond. B, 22 x 28 in $100-200

200. Creature From the Black Lagoon, Universal, 1954, six-sheet, Cond. A-, linenbacked, 81 x 81 in $7,000-9,000

The 1950s brought monsters and robots that often had their origins in outer space. The posters are usually far more memorable than the films themselves.

201. Revenge of the Creature, Universal, 1955, insert, Cond. B-, 36 x 14 in $400-600

202. Tobor the Great, Republic, 1954, three-sheet, Cond. B, linenbacked, 81 x 41 in $900-1,200

203. It Came From Outer Space, Universal, 1953, three-sheet, Cond. B+, linenbacked, 81 x 41 in $700-900

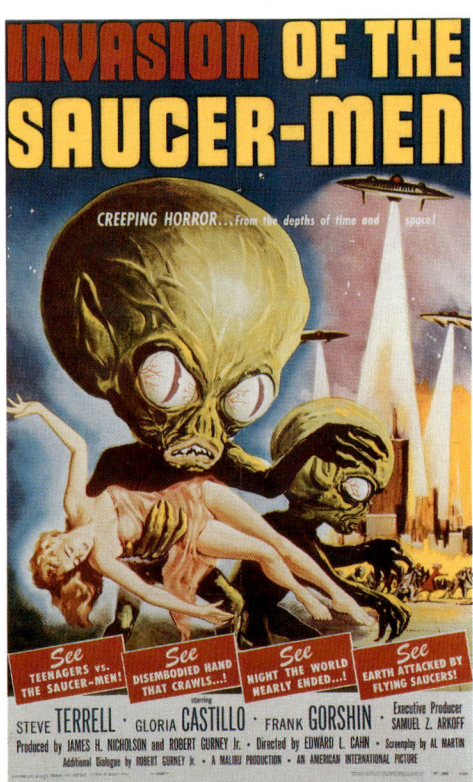

204. Invasion of the Saucer-Men, A.I.P., 1957, one-sheet, Cond. B+, linenbacked, 41 x 27 in $1,000-1,500

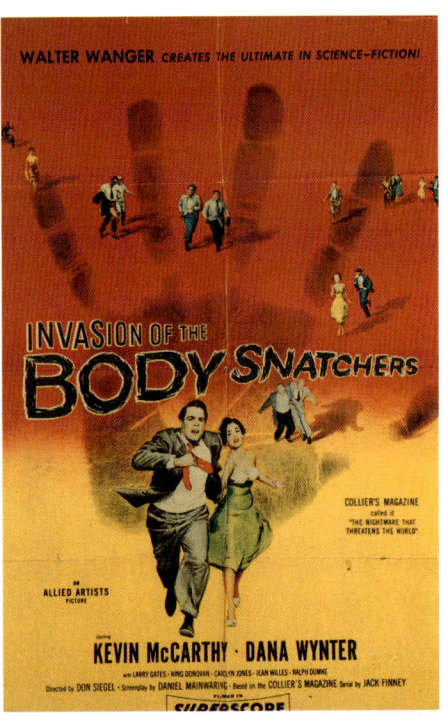

205. Invasion of the Body Snatchers, Allied Artists, 1956, one-sheet, Cond. B, 41 x 27 in $500-700

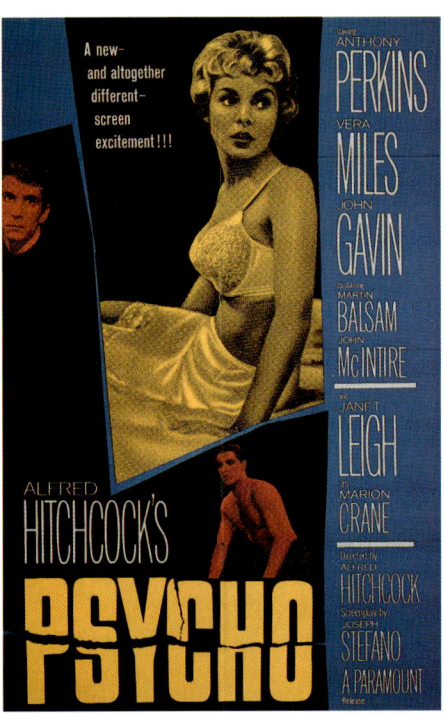

206. Psycho, Paramount, 1960, one-sheet, Cond. A-, 41 x 27 in $500-700

A few of the 1950s science fiction films such as **When Worlds Collide** had intelligent and literate themes, but more often they relied on sensationalism and fears of atomic energy to enthrall their audiences.

207. When Worlds Collide, Paramount, 1951, insert, Cond. B, 36 x 14 in $200-400

208. The Wasp Woman, The Film Group, 1959, half-sheet, Cond. B-, 22 x 28 in $200-400

209. The Blob, Paramount, 1958, one-sheet, Cond. A-, 41 x 27 in $300-500

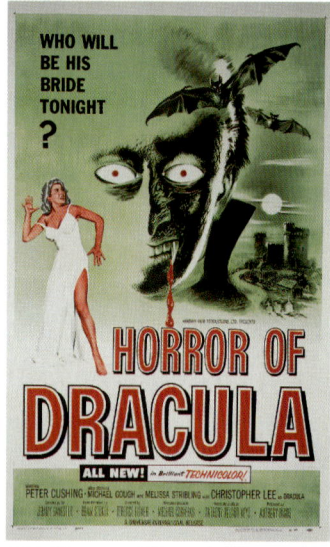

210. Horror of Dracula, Universal, 1958, one-sheet, Cond. B+, linen-backed, 41 x 27 in $300-500

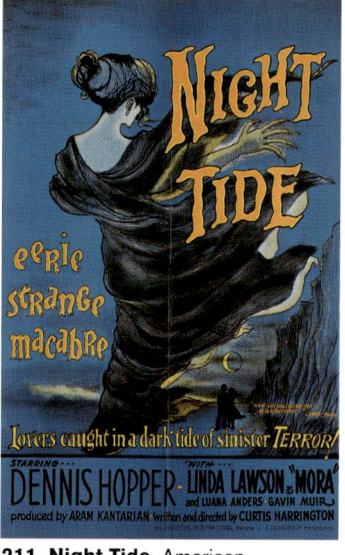

211. Night Tide, American International, 1963, one-sheet, Cond. A, 41 x 27 in $150-300

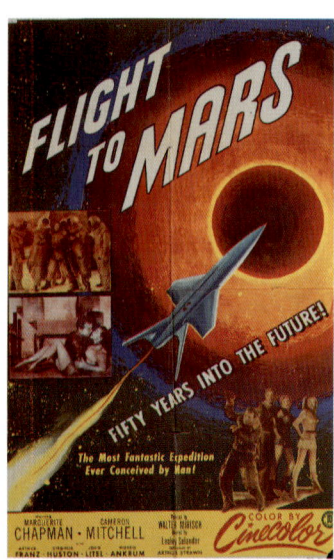

212. Flight to Mars, Monogram, 1951, one-sheet, Cond. B-, 41 x 27 in $300-500

213. It Came From Outer Space, Universal, 1953, window card, Cond. B+, folded, 22 x 14 in $200-400

214. The Horror of Party Beach, 20th Century Fox, 1964, one-sheet, Cond. A, 41 x 27 in $75-150

The middle 1930s saw several drug expose films that are largely viewed as laughable today. The 1960s saw the rise of "bad girl" films, which have a large cult following.

215. Marijuana, Dwain Esper, 1935, Forty by Sixty, Cond. B+, linenbacked, 60 x 40 in $500-700

216. Marihuana, Dwain Esper, 1935, one-sheet, Cond. A-, 41 x 27 in $500-700

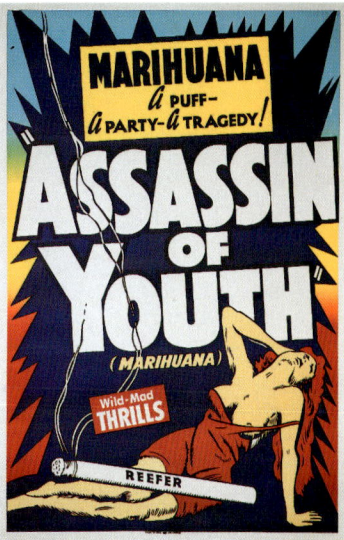

217. Assassin of Youth, BCM Productions, 1937, one-sheet, Cond. B+, linenbacked, 41 x 27 in $500-700

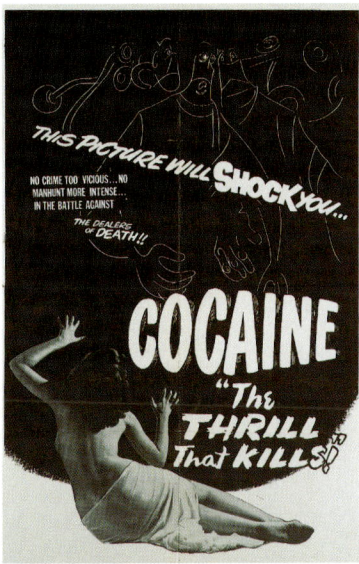

218. Cocaine, studio unknown, circa 1936, one-sheet, Cond. B, 41 x 27 in $400-600

219. Teen Age, Continental Pictures, 1944, one-sheet, Cond. B, linen-backed, 41 x 27 in $200-400

220. Bad Girls Go to Hell, Doris Wishman, 1965, Thirty by Forty, Cond. B+, 40 x 30 in $100-200

221. 4 David Friedman one-sheets, list on request, four one-sheets (one pictured), Cond. A- to B+, each 41 x 27 in $300-500

222. Faster Pussycat! Kill! Kill!, Eve, 1965, style A one-sheet, Cond. B+, 41 x 27 in $400-600

223. Faster Pussycat! Kill! Kill!, Eve, 1965, style B one-sheet, Cond. B+, 41 x 27 in $400-600

Charlie Chaplin began making films in 1914. In a series of short films, he developed a character, The Tramp, that he would play throughout most his career. The three-sheet poster from **The Tramp** is not only the only known copy; it is also the only poster or lobby card known to have survived from this most historic film.

224. The Tramp, Essanay, 1915, three-sheet, Cond. A-, linenbacked, 81 x 41 in
$10,000-15,000

Modern Times was Chaplin's final great silent comedy, made in 1936, long after other filmmakers had abandoned silent filmmaking as outmoded. Many consider it Chaplin's finest film.

225. Modern Times, United Artists, 1936, six-sheet, Cond. B+, linenbacked, 81 x 81 in $10,000-15,000

226. Spite Marriage, MGM, 1929, lobby card, Cond. B+, 11 x 14 in $600-800

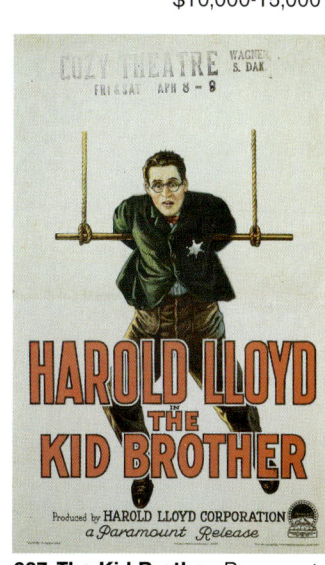

227. The Kid Brother, Paramount, 1927, window card, Cond. B+, folded, 22 x 14 in $200-400

Hal Roach's Our Gang films were extremely popular, but few posters survive from the 1930s. Early in his career, Mickey Rooney made a popular series of Mickey McGuire shorts.

228. Hi-Neighbor, MGM, 1934, one-sheet, Cond. B, linenbacked, 41 x 27 in
$2,000-3,000

229. The Awful Tooth, MGM, 1938, one-sheet, Cond. A-, 41 x 27 in
$1,500-2,000

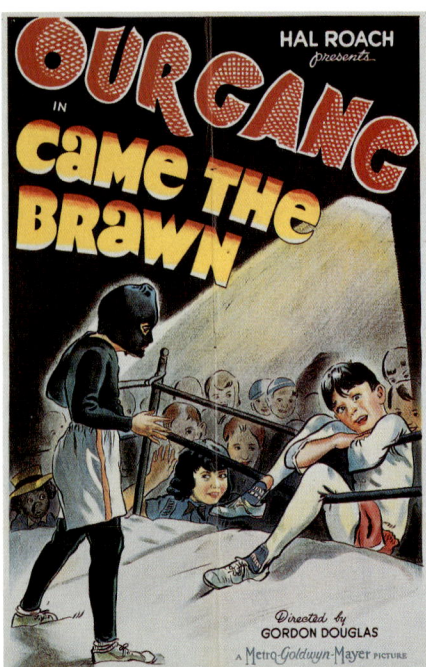

230. Came the Brawn, MGM, 1938, one-sheet, Cond. B, 41 x 27 in $1,500-2,000

231. Our Gang, MGM, circa 1929, one-sheet, Cond. B, paperbacked, 41 x 27 in
$900-1,200

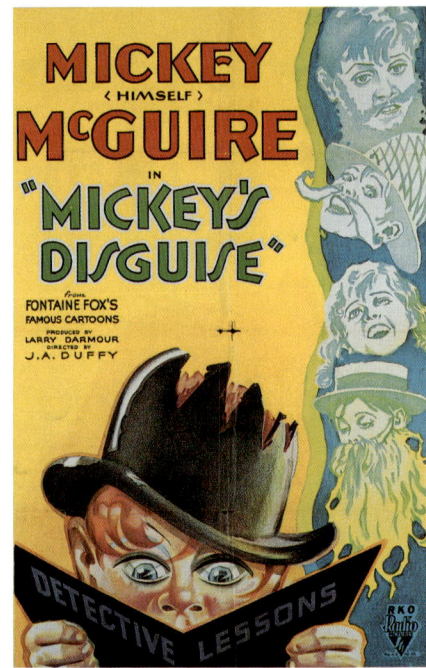

232. Mickey's Disguise, RKO, 1933, one-sheet, Cond. B, 41 x 27 in $500-700

Shirley Temple was certainly the greatest child star of all time. She was Fox's most important star in the mid-1930s, and special posters were made to promote her.

233. Shirley Temple, Fox, 1935, Forty by Sixty, Cond. B+, linenbacked, 60 x 40 in $1,000-1,500

234. Merry X-Mas and a Happy New Year, Fox, 1934, special one-sheet, Cond. B+, linenbacked, 41 x 27 in $1,000-1,500

235. Mickey's Covered Wagon, Columbia, 1933, one-sheet, Cond. B+, 41 x 27 in $500-700

236. Shirley Temple, Fox, 1934, door hanger and standee, Cond. A, 19 x 9 in and 16 x 13 in $200-400

Some silent comedy stars such as W.C. Fields and Charley Chase were able to effectively adapt their methods to sound and continued making films. Comedy short subjects were very popular in the 1930s.

237. Mississippi, Paramount, 1935, one-sheet, Cond. B, linenbacked, 41 x 27 in $800-1,000

238. Poppy, Paramount, 1936, half-sheet, Cond. B, linenbacked, 22 x 28 in $600-800

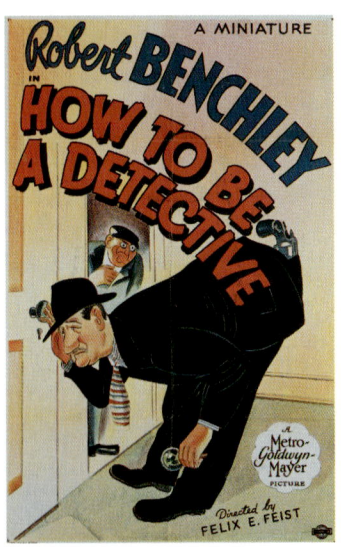

239. How to Be a Detective, MGM, 1936, one-sheet, Cond. A-, 41 x 27 in $700-900

240. I'll Take Vanilla, MGM, 1934, one-sheet, Cond. A-, 41 x 27 in $500-700

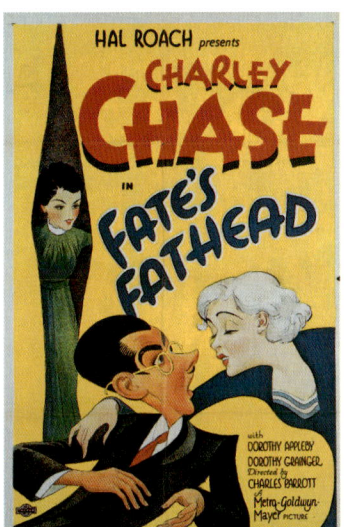

241. Fate's Fathead, MGM, 1934, one-sheet, Cond. B, 41 x 27 in $500-700

242. No More West, RKO, 1934, one-sheet, Cond. A-, 41 x 27 in $600-800

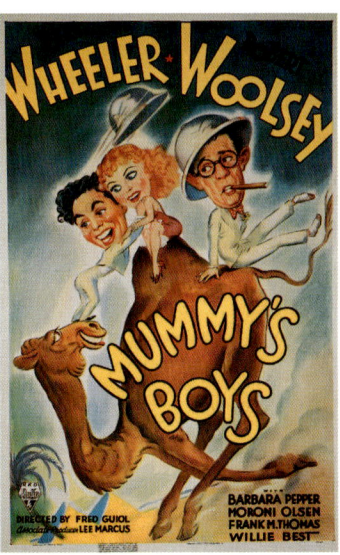

243. Mummy's Boys, RKO, 1936, one-sheet, Cond. B+, linenbacked, 41 x 27 in $500-700

244. The Babbling Book, Paramount, 1932, one-sheet, Cond. B, linenbacked, 41 x 27 in $400-600

Tom Mix was one of the greatest western stars. In 1935, he made **The Miracle Rider**, a serial. The one-sheet poster from each chapter, as well as the three-sheet and set of color lobby cards are offered.

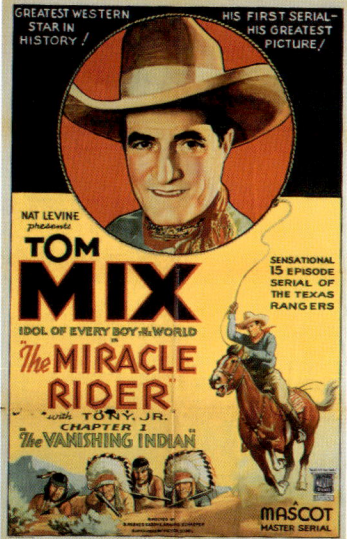

245. The Miracle Rider, Mascot, 1935, fifteen one-sheets (four pictured), eight Chapter 1 lobby cards (two pictured), and three-sheet, Cond. A to B-, each 41 x 27 in, each 11 x 14 in, and 81 x 41 in
$7,000-10,000

Tom Mix posters have been very popular with collectors, but because he made all of his films in the silent and early sound era, they are extremely difficult to obtain.

246. Hidden Gold, Universal, 1932, one-sheet, Cond. B+, 41 x 27 in
$2,500-3,500

247. The Everlasting Whisper, William Fox, 1925, one-sheet, Cond. B+, 41 x 27 in
$2,000-3,000

248. Prairie Trails, William Fox, 1920, one-sheet, Cond. B-, linenbacked, 41 x 27 in
$1,500-2,000

249. The Daredevil, William Fox, 1920, one-sheet, Cond. B-, linenbacked, 41 x 27 in
$1,500-2,000

250. Outlaws of Red River, William Fox, 1927, Danish poster, Cond. A-, unfolded, 33 x 24 in
$800-1,000

The Iron Horse, about the building of the first transcontinental railroad, is one of the most acclaimed silent films. It was directed by the legendary John Ford.

251. The Canyon of Light, William Fox, 1926, Danish poster, Cond. B, linenbacked, 32 x 24 in
$800-1,000

252. The Flaming Frontier, Universal, 1926, one-sheet, Cond. B+, 41 x 27 in
$700-900

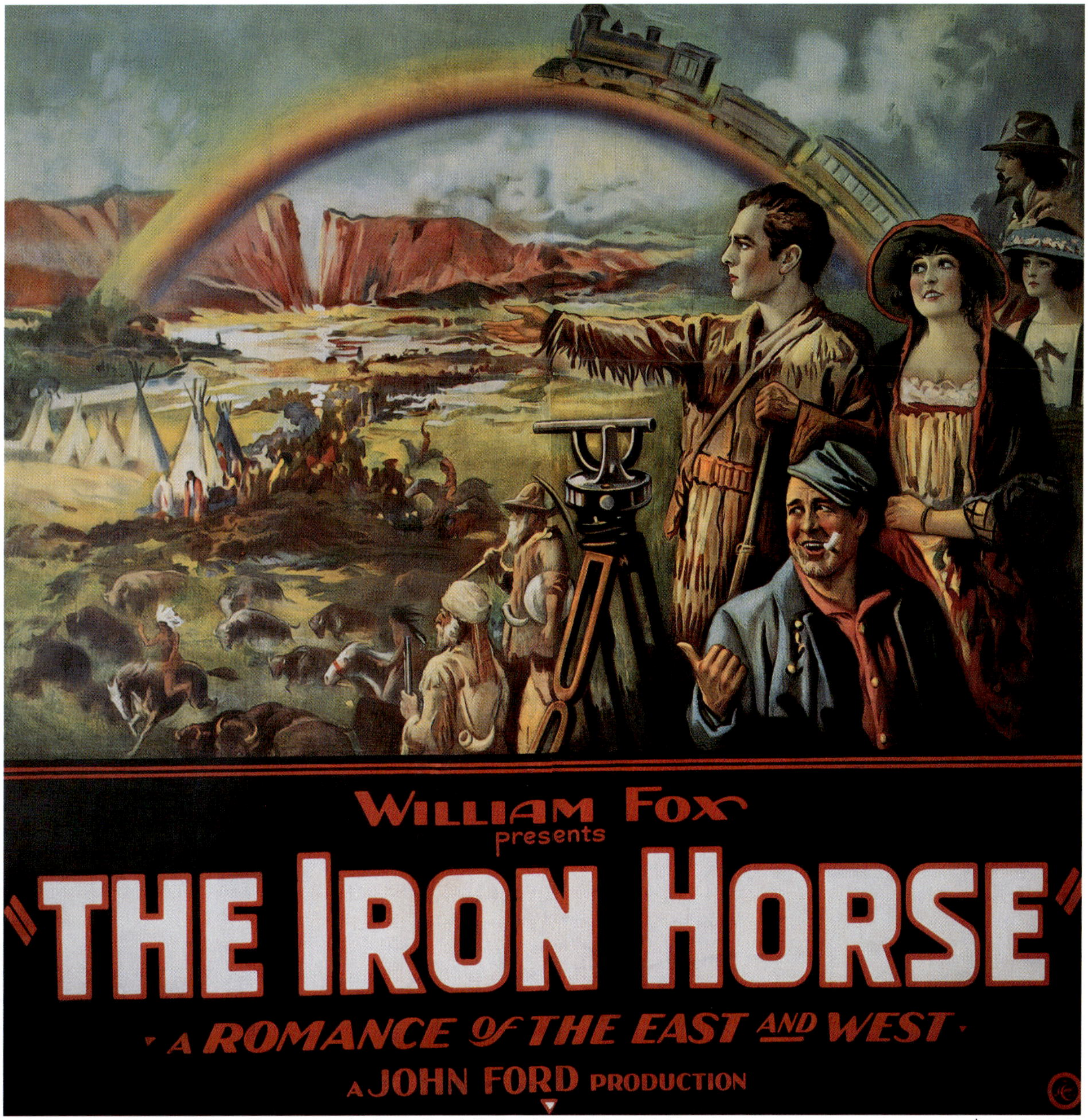

253. The Iron Horse, William Fox, 1924, six-sheet, Cond. B, linenbacked, 81 x 81 in $6,000-9,000

In the 1930s, a one-sheet poster was created for every short subject film, but they are far rarer than those of feature films. In many cases, only a single copy of each is known.

254. Knee-Deep in Music, RKO, 1933, one-sheet, Cond. B+, linen-backed, 41 x 27 in $600-800

255. A Torch Tango, RKO, 1934, one-sheet, Cond. B, 41 x 27 in $500-700

256. If This Isn't Love, RKO, 1934, one-sheet, Cond. A-, 41 x 27 in $500-700

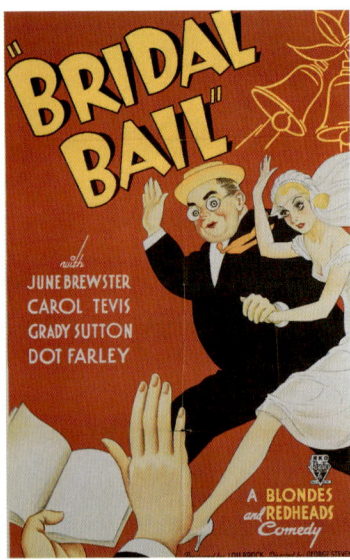

257. Bridal Bail, RKO, 1934, one-sheet, Cond. B+, 41 x 27 in $500-700

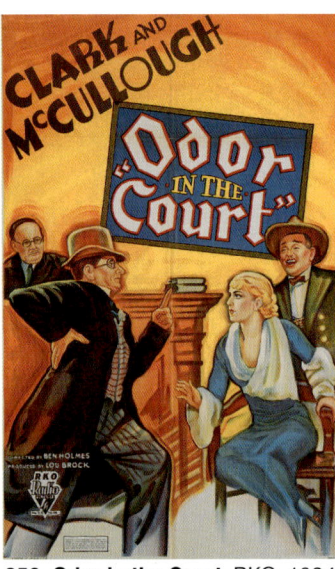

258. Odor in the Court, RKO, 1934, one-sheet, Cond. A-, 41 x 27 in $500-700

259. In-Laws are Out, RKO, 1934, one-sheet, Cond. B+, 41 x 27 in $500-700

260. Major Bowes Amateur Parade, RKO, 1936, one-sheet, Cond. A-, 41 x 27 in $400-600

261. The Story of the Vatican, RKO, 1941, one-sheet, Cond. B+, 41 x 27 in $400-600

262. The March of Time, RKO, circa 1937, one-sheet, Cond. B+, 41 x 27 in $400-600

Mickey Mouse was an instant success. Between 1932 and 1935, United Artists created beautiful full-color posters for his cartoons, and they are the most desired by collectors.

263. Mickey Mouse, Walt Disney, 1932, one-sheet, Cond. B, linenbacked, 41 x 27 in $15,000-20,000

In 1935, Walt Disney began filming in technicolor, and a redesigned version of the earlier **Mickey Mouse** poster was created, prominently announcing the addition of color.

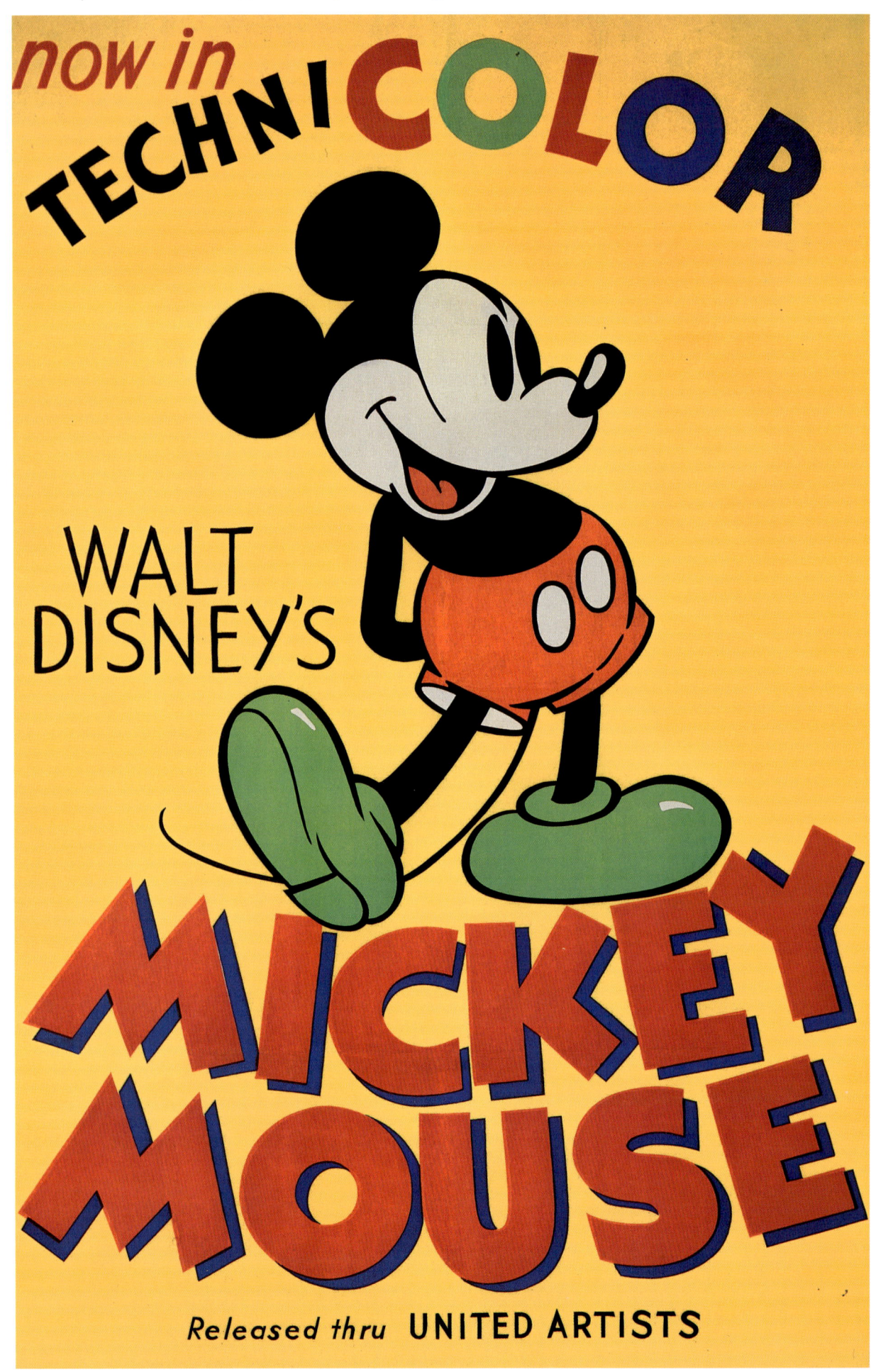

264. Mickey Mouse, Walt Disney, 1935, one-sheet, Cond. B, linenbacked, 41 x 27 in $10,000-15,000

Disney filmed a series of cartoons called **Silly Symphonies.** Few posters for specific entries in this series are known. One of the most charming is the one-sheet poster created for **Bugs in Love.**

265. Bugs in Love, Walt Disney, 1932, one-sheet, Cond. B+, 41 x 27 in $9,000-12,000

Disney would also create generic posters for the **Silly Symphonies** series. The one made in 1934 depicts a new cartoon duck, Donald, who many people would consider one of Disney's finest creations.

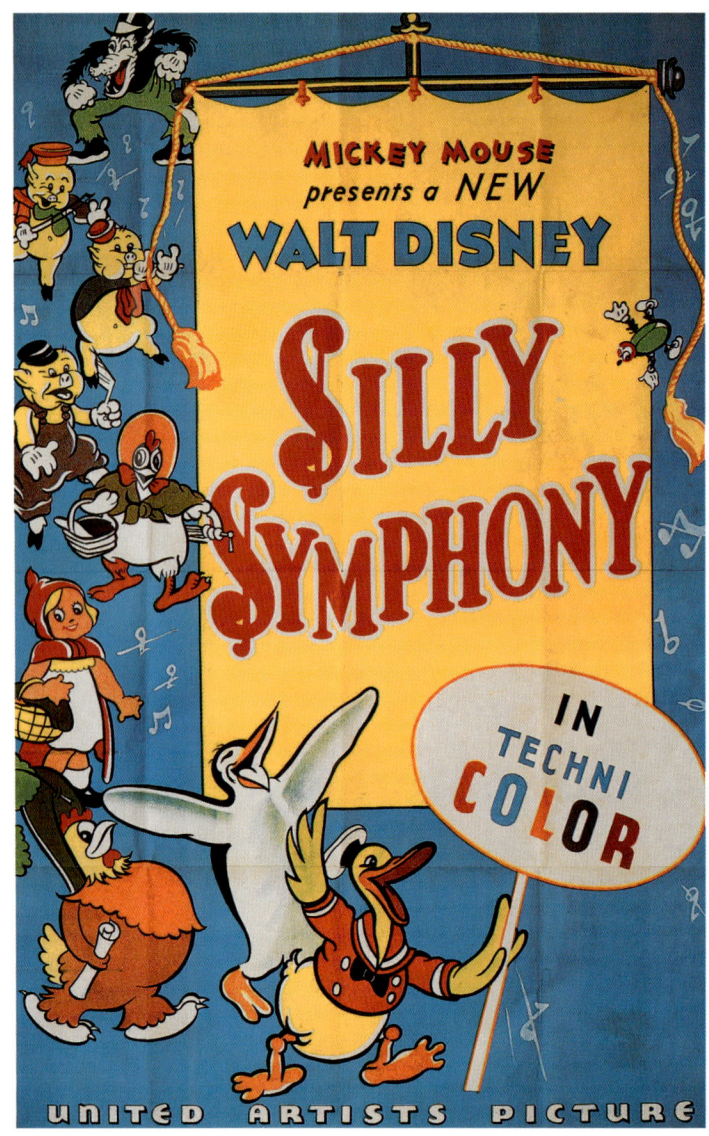

266. Silly Symphony, Walt Disney, 1934, one-sheet, Cond. B+, 41 x 27 in
$7,000-9,000

267. Silly Symphony, Walt Disney, circa 1932, one-sheet, Cond. B, linen-backed, 41 x 27 in
$5,000-7,000

268. The New Spirit, Walt Disney, 1942, one-sheet, Cond. A-, 41 x 27 in $2,000-3,000

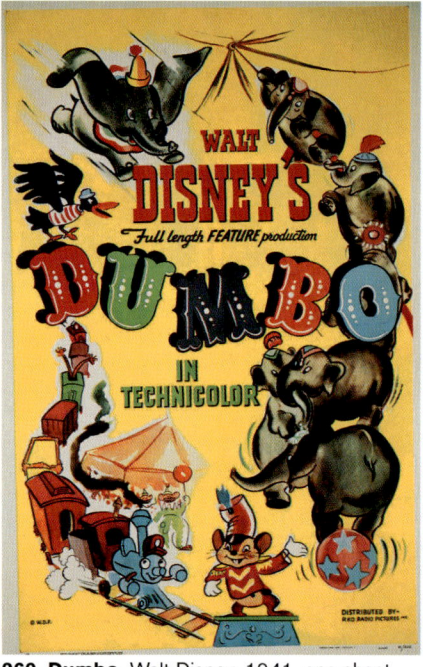

269. Dumbo, Walt Disney, 1941, one-sheet, Cond. B, linenbacked, 41 x 27 in $2,000-3,000

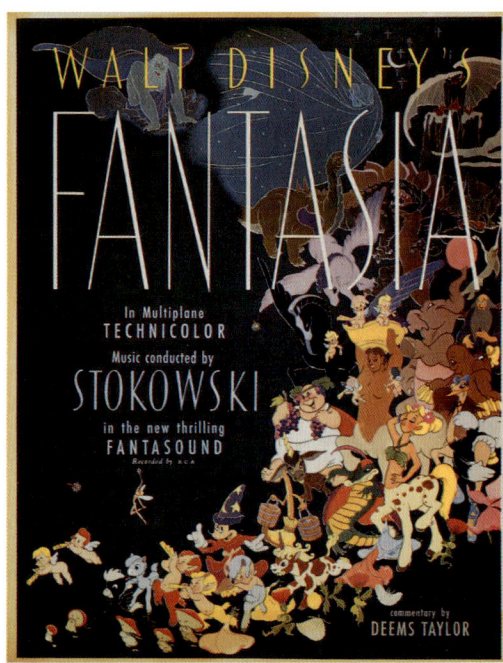

270. Fantasia, Walt Disney, 1940, window card, Cond. B+, trimmed, 18 x 14 in $1,000-1,500

Ferdinand the Bull was one of the best of the Silly Symphonies, and it deservedly won an Academy Award. Films such as these are still being watched and loved by children everywhere.

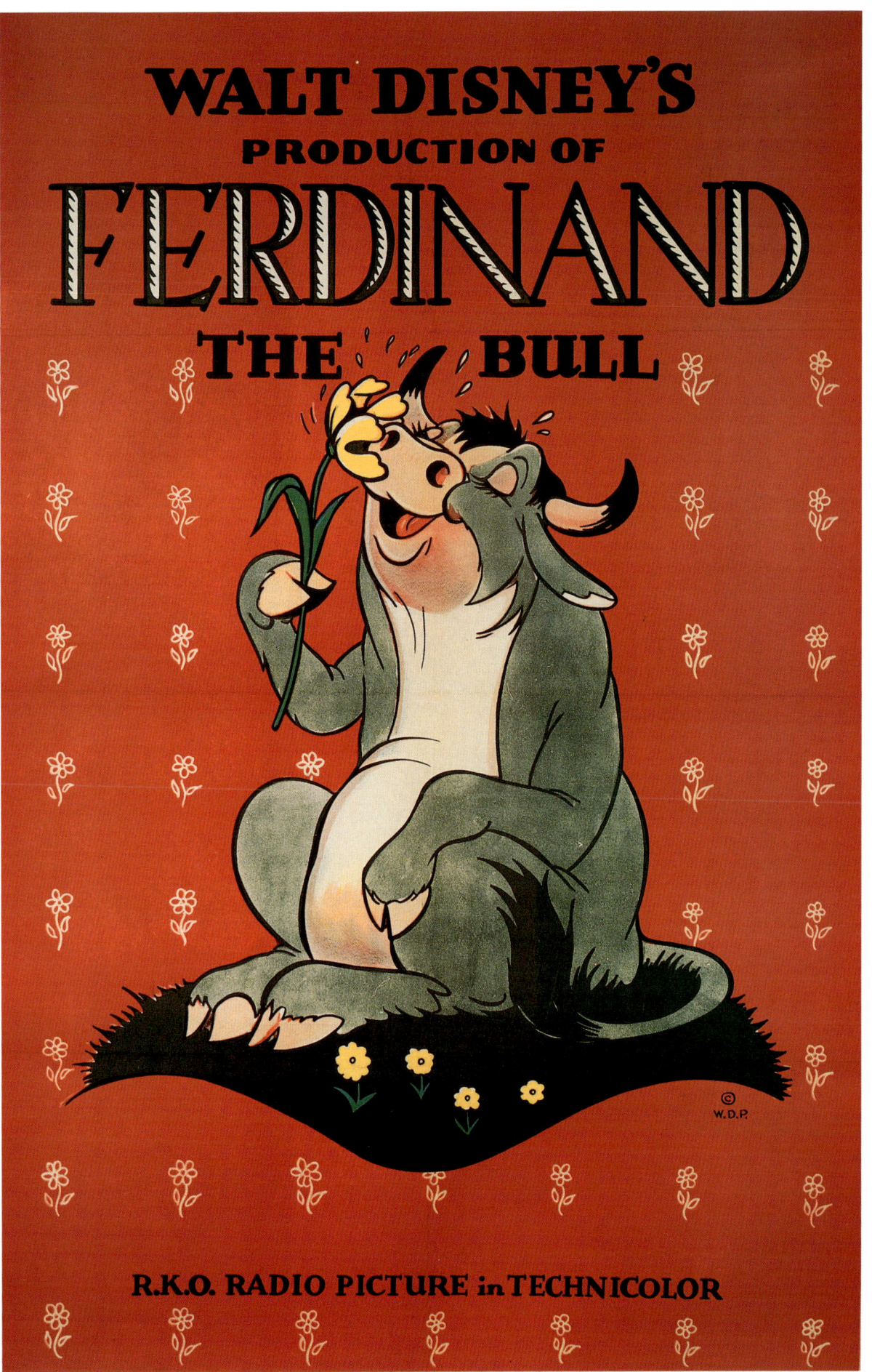

271. Ferdinand the Bull, Walt Disney, 1938, one-sheet, Cond. B+, linenbacked, 41 x 27 in $10,000-15,000

After the success of **Snow White**, Walt Disney made a long string of highly successful cartoon features, sometimes mixing live-action with animation.

272. Pinocchio, Walt Disney, 1954 reissue, one-sheet, Cond. A-, 41 x 27 in $400-600

273. The Reluctant Dragon, Walt Disney, 1941, one-sheet, Cond. B+, linenbacked, 41 x 27 in $500-700

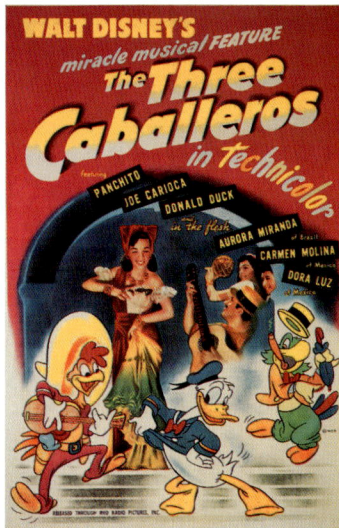

274. The Three Caballeros, Walt Disney, 1944, one-sheet, Cond. B, linenbacked, 41 x 27 in $600-800

275. Song of the South, Walt Disney, 1946, one-sheet, Cond. B, linenbacked, 41 x 27 in $400-600

276. Make Mine Music, Walt Disney, 1946, one-sheet, Cond. B+, linenbacked, 41 x 27 in $400-600

277. Fun and Fancy Free, Walt Disney, 1947, one-sheet, Cond. B+, linenbacked, 41 x 27 in $500-700

278. Melody Time, Walt Disney, 1948, one-sheet, Cond. B, linenbacked, 41 x 27 in $400-600

279. Cinderella, Walt Disney, 1950, one-sheet, Cond. B, linenbacked, 41 x 27 in $500-700

280. Pluto's Party, Walt Disney, 1952, one-sheet, Cond. B+, 41 x 27 in $400-600

Disney mainly made animated films in the 1950s and 1960s, but also made live-action films. Two of the best-remembered are **Davy Crockett, King of the Wild Frontier**, and **Old Yeller**.

281. Peter Pan, Walt Disney, 1953, one-sheet, Cond. B, linenbacked, 41 x 27 in $500-700

282. Davy Crockett, King of the Wild Frontier, Walt Disney, 1955, set of eight lobby cards (one pictured), Cond. A-, each 11 x 14 in $300-500

283. Lady and the Tramp, Walt Disney, 1955, one-sheet, Cond. B-, linenbacked, 41 x 27 in $600-800

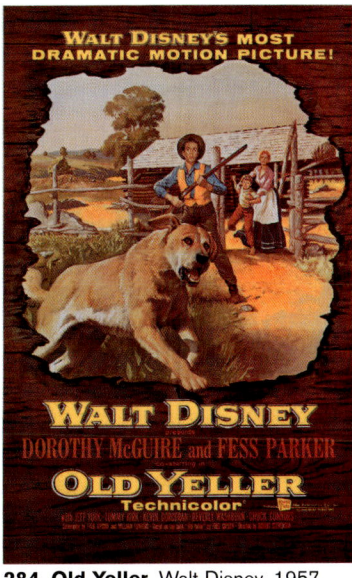

284. Old Yeller, Walt Disney, 1957, one-sheet, Cond. B+, 41 x 27 in $200-300

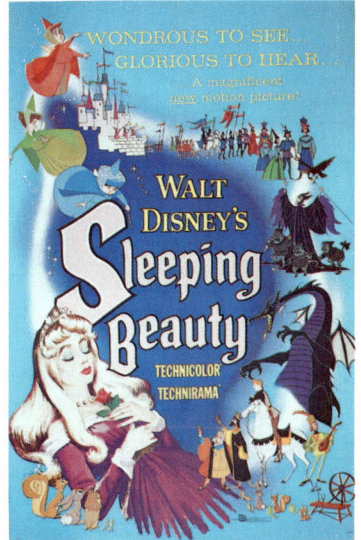

285. Sleeping Beauty, Walt Disney, 1959, one-sheet, Cond. B, linenbacked, 41 x 27 in $500-700

286. One Hundred and One Dalmatians, Walt Disney, 1961, one-sheet, Cond. B, linenbacked, 41 x 27 in $500-700

287. Gala Day at Disneyland, Walt Disney, 1960, one-sheet, Cond. B+, 41 x 27 in $400-600

288. Disneyland After Dark, Walt Disney, 1962, one-sheet, Cond. B+, linenbacked, 41 x 27 in $300-500

Marilyn Monroe quicky shot to stardom, after bit parts in films such as **Love Happy**. The best posters and lobby cards from many of her finest films are offered.

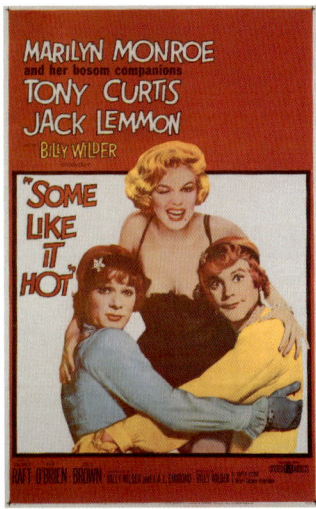

289. Some Like It Hot, United Artists, 1959, one-sheet, Cond. B, linenbacked, 41 x 27 in $600-800

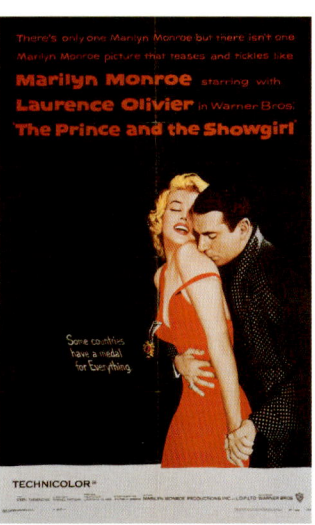

290. The Prince and the Showgirl, Warner Brothers, 1957, one-sheet, Cond. A-, 41 x 27 in $500-700

291. Bus Stop, 20th Century Fox, 1956, one-sheet, Cond. B+, linen-backed, 41 x 27 in $300-500

292. Love Happy, United Artists, 1949, lobby card, Cond. B+, 11 x 14 in $500-700

293. The Prince and the Showgirl, Warner Brothers, 1957, lobby card, Cond. B+, 11 x 14 in $300-500

294. Niagara, 20th Century Fox, 1952, half-sheet, Cond. B, 22 x 28 in $400-600

295. A Place in the Sun, Paramount, 1951, set of eight lobby cards (one pictured), Cond. A, each 11 x 14 in $500-700

Elvis Presley's first film was **Love Me Tender**, and he quickly became one of the most popular stars of the 1960s. One of his most popular films was **Viva Las Vegas**, with Ann-Margret.

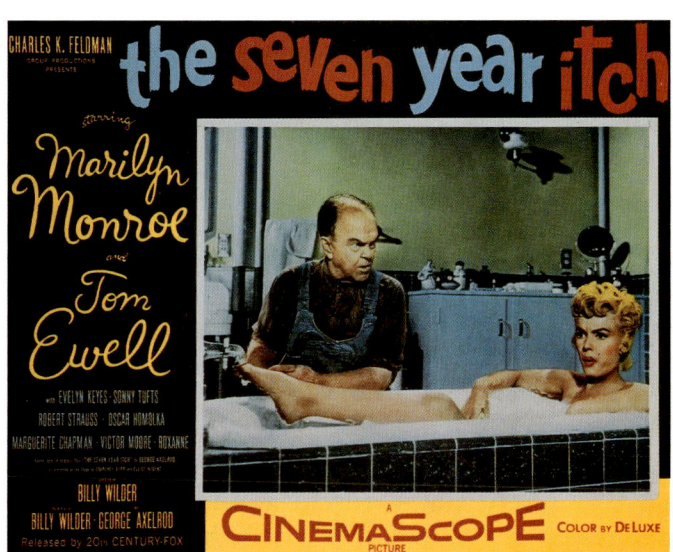

296. 15 Marilyn Monroe lobby cards, list on request, fifteen lobby cards (four pictured), Cond. A- to B, each 11 x 14 in $1,000-2,000

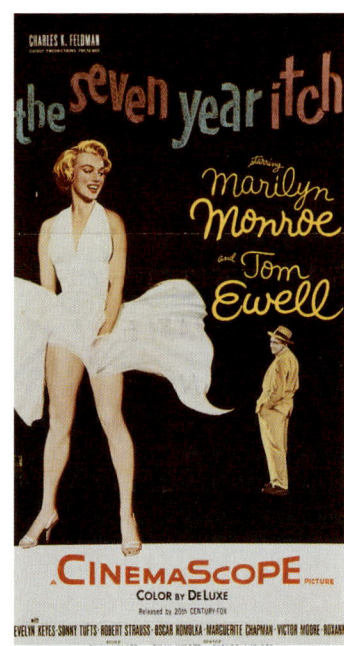

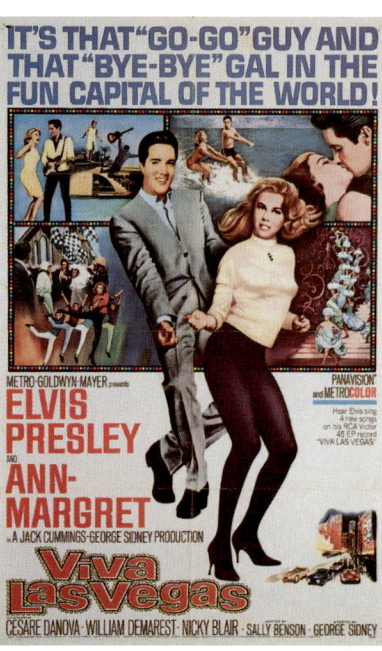

297. The Seven Year Itch, 20th Century Fox, 1955, insert, Cond. B-, 36 x 14 in $300-500

298. Love Me Tender, 20th Century Fox, 1956, one-sheet, Cond. A-, 41 x 27 in $400-600

299. Viva Las Vegas, MGM, 1964, one-sheet, Cond. B, 41 x 27 in $400-600

James Dean only made three films before his untimely death in a car crash, yet he became a major teen idol whose star remains undiminished after forty years.

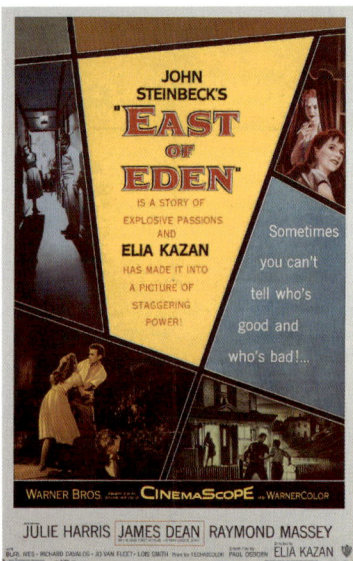

300. 3 James Dean one-sheets, Warner Brothers, 1955-56, three one-sheets, Cond. A, A-, and B+, each 41 x 27 in $2,000-3,000

301. Rebel Without a Cause, Warner Brothers, 1955, Argentinian poster, Cond. B, linenbacked, 41 x 27 in
$500-700

302. Giant, Warner Brothers, 1956, lobby card, Cond. B-, 11 x 14 in
$100-200

Some studios such as Paramount would give a name to each type of its short subjects and then create elaborate generic full-color one-sheets to promote each series.

303. The Unemployed Ghost, Paramount, 1931, one-sheet, Cond. A-, 41 x 27 in $500-700

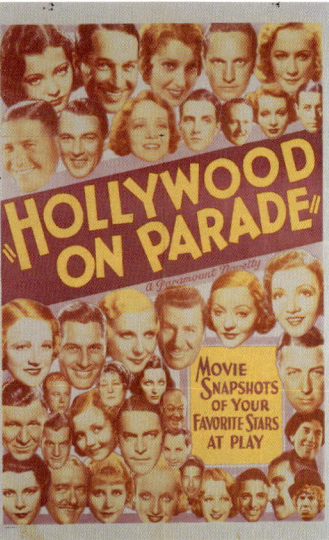

304. Hollywood on Parade, Paramount, 1932, one-sheet, Cond. B, 41 x 27 in $400-600

305. Paramount Pictorial, Paramount, 1936, one-sheet, Cond. B, linenbacked, 41 x 27 in $400-600

306. Paramount Paragraphics, Paramount, 1936, one-sheet, Cond. B, 41 x 27 in $400-600

307. Paramount on Parade Around the World, Paramount, 1938, one-sheet, Cond. A-, 41 x 27 in $400-600

308. Screen Souvenirs, Paramount, circa 1935, one-sheet, Cond. B, 41 x 27 in $400-600

309. La Savate, MGM, circa 1938, one-sheet, Cond. B, linenbacked, 41 x 27 in $500-700

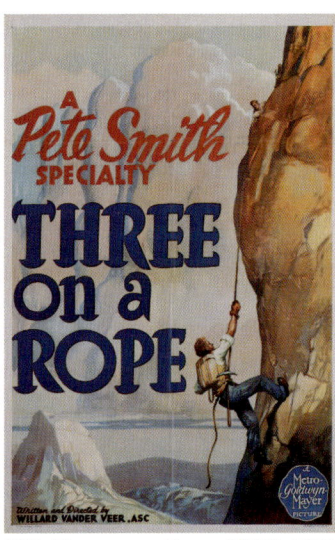

310. Three on a Rope, MGM, 1938, one-sheet, Cond. A-, 41 x 27 in $400-600

311. Red Men On Parade, MGM, 1940, one-sheet, Cond. B, linenbacked, 41 x 27 in $400-600

The posters from the earliest 1930s Three Stooges comedy shorts are extremely rare and prized by collectors. The one-sheet offered from **Woman Haters** is not only the very first film the Stooges made for Columbia Pictures, but it is also believed to be the only copy known.

312. Woman Haters, Columbia, 1934, one-sheet, Cond. B+, 41 x 27 in $20,000-30,000

Most Columbia Three Stooges posters depict photographic images (**Woman Haters** is a happy exception), and all are two-color. **Grips, Grunts and Groans** has one of the best images of all the 1930s Three Stooges posters, featuring large images of the comedy trio.

313. Grips, Grunts and Groans, Columbia, 1937, one-sheet, Cond. B+, 41 x 27 in $9,000-12,000

B-westerns were a mainstay of Columbia and Universal in the 1930s, and they often promoted them with beautifully designed one-sheets that are prized by collectors.

314. Silent Men, Columbia, 1933, one-sheet, Cond. B, linenbacked, 41 x 27 in
$900-1,200

315. Sunset of Power, Universal, 1936, one-sheet, Cond. B, linenbacked, 41 x 27 in
$900-1,200

316. The Western Code, Columbia, 1932, one-sheet, Cond. B, linenbacked, 41 x 27 in
$500-700

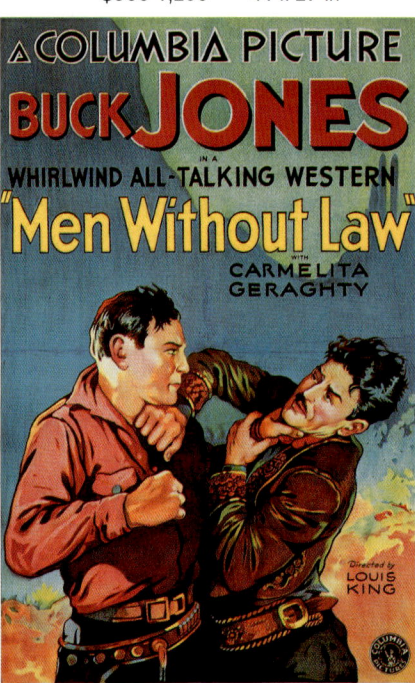

317. Men Without Law, Columbia, 1930, one-sheet, Cond. B, linenbacked, 41 x 27 in
$700-900

318. Left Handed Law, Universal, 1937, one-sheet, Cond. B, linenbacked, 41 x 27 in
$700-900

Buck Jones was the foremost cowboy star at Columbia, and later Universal. John Wayne spent much of the 1930s making B-Westerns for tiny Republic Studios.

319. Silver Spurs, Universal, 1936, one-sheet, Cond. B, linenbacked, 41 x 27 in $900-1,200

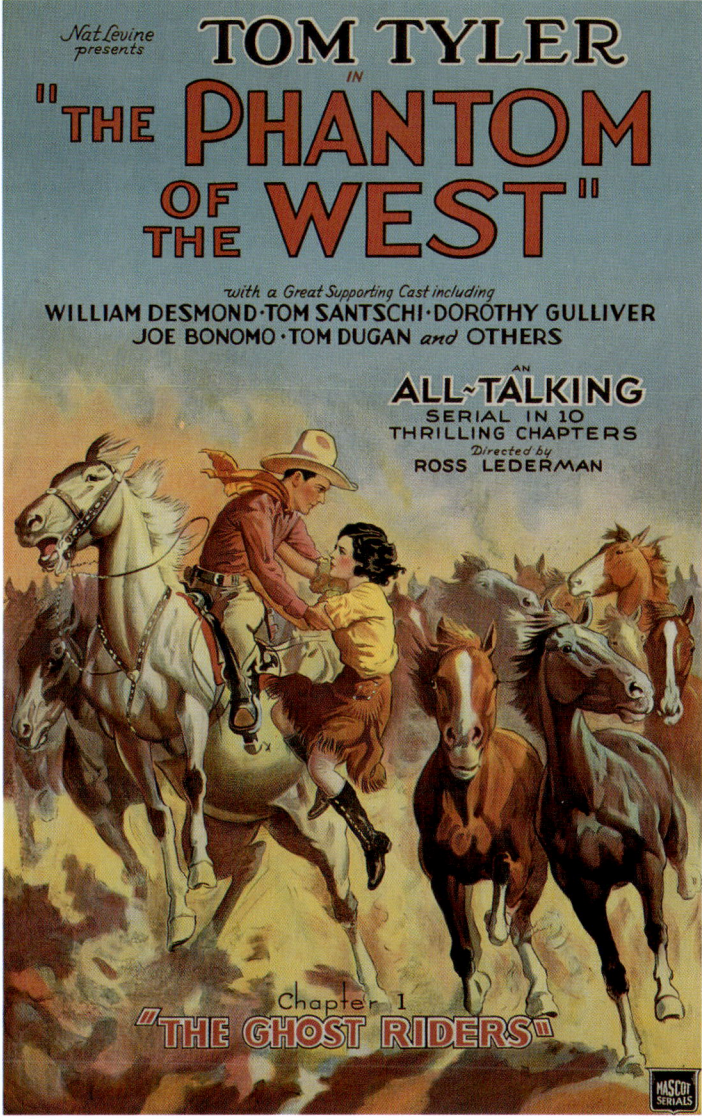

320. The Phantom of the West, Mascot, 1934, one-sheet, Cond. B+, 41 x 27 in $700-900

321. Deep in the Heart of Texas, Universal, 1942, one-sheet, Cond. B, 41 x 27 in $200-400

322. Santa Fe Trail, Warner Brothers, 1940, one-sheet, Cond. B-, linenbacked, 41 x 27 in $600-800

323. New Frontier, Republic, 1939, one-sheet, Cond. B, linenbacked, 41 x 27 in $700-900

In 1938, Roy Rogers made his first films for Republic Studios, and he quickly became a major star. Audiences loved him, and he made many highly popular films in the 1940s.

324. Saga of Death Valley, Republic, 1940, one-sheet, Cond. B-, linenbacked, signed by Roy Rogers, 41 x 27 in
$1,000-1,500

325. Shine on Harvest Moon, Republic, 1938, one-sheet, Cond. B, linenbacked, 41 x 27 in
$900-1,200

326. Frontier Pony Express, Republic, 1939, one-sheet, Cond. B-, linenbacked, 41 x 27 in
$700-900

327. Heart of the Golden West, Republic, 1942, one-sheet, Cond. B, 41 x 27 in
$400-600

328. Romance on the Range, Republic, 1942, one-sheet, Cond. B+, linenbacked, 41 x 27 in
$400-600

It didn't matter to Roy's loyal fans that the plots of many of his films were virtually the same. Roy was a true American hero!

329. Jesse James at Bay, Republic, 1941, one-sheet, Cond. B, linenbacked, 41 x 27 in $800-1,000

330. South of Santa Fe, Republic, 1942, one-sheet, Cond. B+, 41 x 27 in $600-800

331. Bells of Rosarita, Republic, 1945, one-sheet, Cond. B+, 41 x 27 in $300-500

332. Springtime in the Sierras, Republic, 1947, one-sheet, Cond. B+, 41 x 27 in $300-500

333. 8 Roy Rogers lobby cards, Republic, 1930s and 1940s, list on request, 8 lobby cards (two pictured), Cond. B to B-, each 11 x 14 in $200-400

Gene Autry and Hopalong Cassidy were the other major B-western stars of the 1940s. Gene made his films at Republic, while Hoppy's films were from Paramount, and later United Artists.

334. Trail Dust, Paramount, 1936, one-sheet, Cond. B, linenbacked, 41 x 27 in
$600-800

335. Rootin' Tootin' Rhythm, Republic, 1937, one-sheet, Cond. B-, linenbacked, 41 x 27 in
$700-900

336. Melody Ranch, Republic, 1940, one-sheet, Cond. B, linenbacked, 41 x 27 in
$500-700

337. 8 Gene Autry lobby cards, Republic, 1930s and 1940s, list on request, 8 lobby cards (one pictured), Cond. A- to B, each 11 x 14 in
$200-400

The 1950s saw the slow end of B-westerns, but two of the finest and most-loved major western films ever, **High Noon** and **Shane,** were made at this time.

338. High Noon, United Artists, 1952, one-sheet, Cond. B+, 41 x 27 in
$1,000-1,500

339. Shane, Paramount, 1953, Italian poster, Cond. B+, linenbacked, 78 x 55 in
$700-1,000

340. Red River, United Artists, 1948, British quad and Pressbook, Cond. A-, 30 x 40 in and 12 x 9 in
$600-800

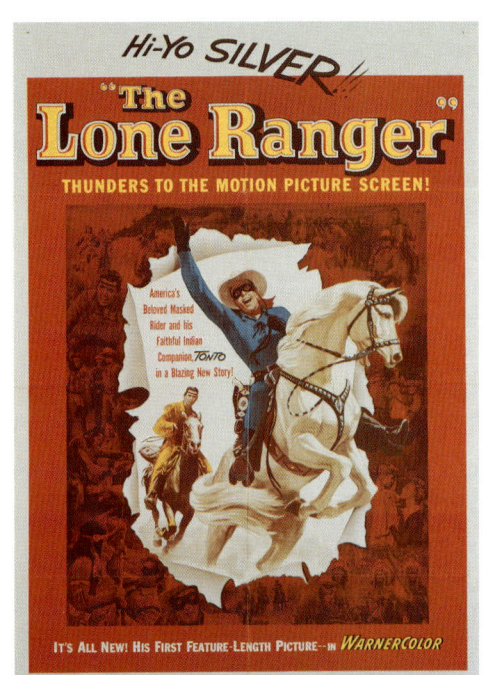

341. The Lone Ranger, Warner Brothers, 1956, one-sheet, Cond. A-, 41 x 27 in
$400-600

Clint Eastwood single-handedly revived the cowboy genre with a series of films in the 1960s and 1970s. The first of these were filmed in Italy, and were dubbed "spaghetti westerns".

342. For a Few Dollars More, PEA, 1965, Italian poster, Cond. B+, linenbacked, 78 x 55 in $1,000-1,500

343. Winchester '73, Universal, 1950, insert, Cond. B, paperbacked, 36 x 14 in $400-600

344. High Plains Drifter, Universal, 1972, half-sheet, Cond. A-, 22 x 28 in $100-200

345. The Outlaw Josey Wales, Warner Brothers, 1976, one-sheet, Cond. A, 41 x 27 in $100-200

346. Superman and the Molemen, Lippert, 1951, insert, Cond. B+, 36 x 14 in
$1,500-2,000

348. Atom Man vs. Superman, Columbia, 1950, one-sheet, Cond. B, linenbacked, 41 x 27 in $1,000-1,500

347. Valley of the Cliffhangers limited edition book, Jack Mathis,1975, Cond. A-, 18 x12 in $1,000-1,500

349. Zorro Rides Again, Republic, 1937, one-sheet, Cond. B, linenbacked, 41 x 27 in $700-900

350. The Vigilantes are Coming, Republic, 1936, one-sheet, Cond. B+, linenbacked, 41 x 27 in $700-900

Every visit to a Saturday matinee in the 1930s and 1940s included at least one chapter of an action-packed serial. **Superman and the Molemen** played in theaters, and was used as a two part pilot episode for the highly successful TV series.

African-Americans were largely denied roles in mainstream U.S. films until the 1960s, and they made their own films that were shown primarily to black audiences.

351. 30 black cast lobby cards, 1930s to 1950s, list on request, 30 lobby cards (four pictured), Cond. A- to B-, each 11 x 14 in $1,500-3,000

352. The Fight Never Ends, Alexander, 1949, set of eight lobby cards (one pictured), Cond. B to C+, each 11 x 14 in $200-400

353. Pinky, 20th Century Fox, 1949, one-sheet, Cond. B, linenbacked, 41 x 27 in $400-600

One of director Fred Zinnemann's first films was a short subject about the famed Dr. Carver. The **Sports Cavalcade** poster pictures three of the most famous black athletes of all time.

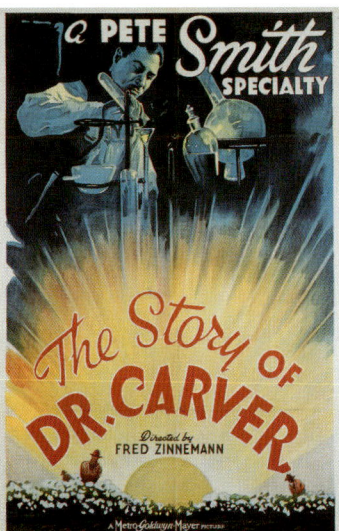

354. The Story of Dr. Carver, MGM, 1938, one-sheet, Cond. A-, 41 x 27 in
$400-600

355. Harlem Rides the Range, Sack, 1939, one-sheet, Cond. B+, linen-backed, 41 x 27 in
$700-900

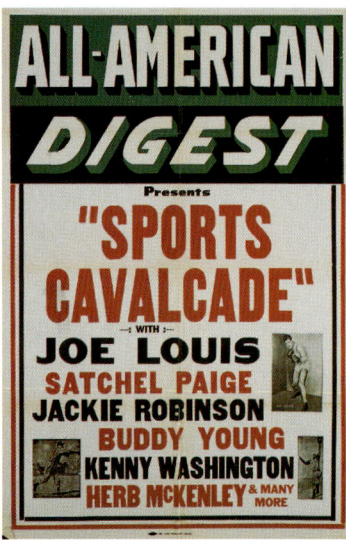

356. Sports Cavalcade, All-American, circa 1948, one-sheet, Cond. B+, 41 x 27 in
$500-700

357. While Thousands Cheer, Popkin, 1940, one-sheet, Cond. B+, 41 x 27 in
$300-500

358. Up Jumped the Devil, Toddy, circa 1945, one-sheet, Cond. B, 41 x 27 in
$300-500

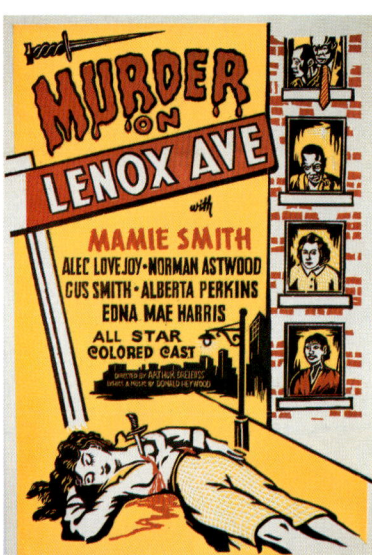

359. Murder on Lenox Ave, Colonnade, 1941, one-sheet, Cond. B, linenbacked, 41 x 27 in
$600-800

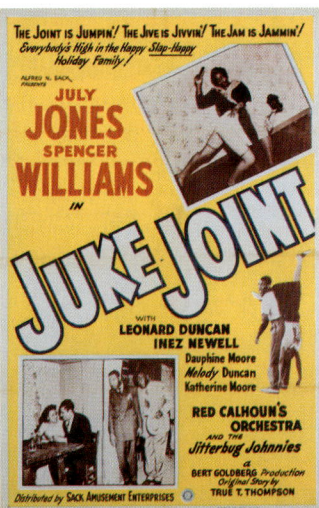

360. Juke Joint, Sack, 1947, one-sheet, Cond. B+, 41 x 27 in
$500-700

361. Rock 'N Roll Revue, Studio Films, 1955, one-sheet, Cond. B, linenbacked, 41 x 27 in
$400-600

362. Rhythm and Blues Revue, Studio Films, 1955, one-sheet, Cond. B, linenbacked, 41 x 27 in
$400-600

363. The Wizard of Oz, MGM, 1939, half-sheet, Cond. B-, paperbacked, 22 x 28 in $9,000-12,000

364. The Wizard of Oz, MGM, 1939, two door hangers, Cond. A-, each 21 x 10 in $900-1,200

Everyone agrees that **The Wizard of Oz** is one of the finest films ever made. Offered here are two extremely rare original posters, as well as two previously unknown door hangers.

366. The Wizard of Oz, MGM, 1949 reissue, one-sheet, Cond. B, linenbacked, 41 x 27 in　　　　　　$700-900

367. The Wizard of Oz, MGM, 1955 reissue, insert, Cond. B+, 36 x 14 in　　$500-700

365. The Wizard of Oz, MGM, 1939, insert, Cond. B-, paperbacked, 36 x 14 in　　　　　　$7,000-9,000

Exotic locales and animals have always appealed to filmmakers. **Mighty Joe Young** was the first film of Ray Harryhausen, and was made with the help of Willis O'Brien, creator of King Kong.

368. East of Borneo, Universal, 1931, one-sheet, Cond. B+, linenbacked, 41 x 27 in $1,000-1,500

369. The Jungle Book, United Artists, 1942, one-sheet, Cond. B+, 41 x 27 in $500-700

370. You Can Be Had, Universal, 1936, one-sheet, Cond. A-, 41 x 27 in $400-600

371. Mighty Joe Young, RKO, 1949, half-sheet, Cond. B+, 22 x 28 in $400-600

This auction was organized by Bruce Hershenson and Howard Lowery

Bruce Hershenson is the world's foremost vintage movie poster dealer. He has sold movie posters full-time since 1989, and from 1990 to 1997 he was Christie's auction house's movie poster expert, organizing ten movie poster auctions with cumulative sales of nine million dollars. In December, 1998, he organized an auction with Howard Lowery which sold $750,000 of movie posters. He has issued 15 semi-annual sales lists, with cumulative sales of over three million dollars. He has published 19 full-color books of movie poster reproductions. Together with partner Richard Allen, Bruce owns the Hershenson-Allen Archive, which contains over 30,000 color transparencies of vintage movie posters, covering all years and subjects, available for use in books, magazines or videos. Bruce's website, http://www.brucehershenson.com is the most visited vintage movie poster site on the Internet. It contains hundreds of free images of great movie posters, and is packed with information every collector needs to know. If you are looking to buy or sell movie posters, or if you would like free brochures about the books Bruce has published, you can contact him in any of the following ways:

Mail: Bruce Hershenson, P.O. Box 874, West Plains, MO 65775
Phone: 417 256-9616   Fax: 417 257-6948
E-Mail: mail@brucehershenson.com
Website: http://www.brucehershenson.com

Howard Lowery is the owner of Howard Lowery Gallery in Burbank, California, and since the early 1970s has specialized in handling animation art and collectibles. For the past ten years he has produced major auctions with a world-wide following, resulting in highly successful sales of animation art from Disney and all major studios, comic strip art, comic books, Disneyana, movie memorabilia, movie posters, Disneyland attraction posters, and all kinds of collectibles. If you have items you would like to consign to a future Howard Lowery auction, please send a description of your item(s) to 3818 W. Magnolia Blvd, Burbank, CA 91505. If you are interested in purchasing art or collectibles, please contact the Gallery to be notified of upcoming auctions.

This auction will be held at the Feldman Gallery of the PACIFIC DESIGN CENTER in Beverly Hills, California. Directions to the Pacific Design Center are as follows:

We are located at the intersection of San Vicente Blvd. and Melrose Ave. Enter the Parking structure at either Melrose Ave. or San Vicente Blvd. Enter at San Vicente Blvd. only after 5 pm, Monday - Friday

Directions from the following Freeways:

1. Harbor Freeway (11) - Southeast of PDC (from either direction). Harbor Freeway to Santa Monica Freeway (10) West. EXIT at La Cienega Blvd North - Proceed 5 miles. LEFT at Melrose Ave. - PDC is 3 miles down on the right.

2. Hollywood Freeway (101) - East of PDC (from either direction). EXIT at Highland Ave. South - Proceed 2 miles. RIGHT at Melrose Ave. - PDC is 3 miles down on the right.

3. Pasadena Freeway (110) - Northeast of PDC. From Pasadena - Pasadena Freeway (110) to Hollywood Freeway (101) North. EXIT at Melrose Ave. West - Proceed 5 miles PDC is on the right.

4. San Diego Freeway (405) - West of PDC (from either direction). EXIT at Santa Monica Blvd. East - Proceed 5 miles. RIGHT at San Vicente Blvd. - PDC is 2 blocks down on the left.

5. Santa Monica Freeway (10) - South of PDC (from either direction). EXIT at La Cienega Blvd. North - Proceed 5 miles. LEFT at Melrose Ave. - PDC is 3 blocks down on the right.

6. Santa Ana Freeway (5) - Southeast of PDC. Santa Ana Freeway North to Santa Monica Freeway (10) West. EXIT at La Cienega Blvd. North - Proceed 5 miles. LEFT at Melrose Ave. - PDC is 3 blocks down on the right.

7. Ventura Freeway (134) - Northeast of PDC (Glendale) via Laurel Canyon. Venture Freeway (134) North becomes Ventura Freeway (101). EXIT at Laurel Canyon Ave. South - Proceed 5 miles through the canyon. At Sunset Blvd. Laurel Canyon becomes Crescent Heights Blvd. - Proceed 1 mile. RIGHT at Melrose Ave. - Proceed 1 mile PDC is on the right.

8. Venture Freeway (101) - Northwest of PDC (Encino) via San Diego Freeway East or West of San Diego Freeway - to San Diego Freeway South. EXIT at Santa Monica Blvd East - Proceed RIGHT at San Vicente Blvd. - PDC is 1 block down on the left.

9. Ventura Freeway (101) - at North of PDC (Studio City) via Hollywood Freeway Ventura Freeway South becomes Hollywood Freeway (101) South. EXIT at Highland Ave. South - Proceed 2 miles. RIGHT at Melrose Ave. - PDC is 3 miles down on the right.

If you have any special needs related to this auction (bidding, previews, and so forth) please contact either Howard Lowery or Bruce Hershenson, and they will do everything possible to accommodate you.

Vintage Hollywood Posters II Index

The Adventures of Robin Hood 55
Adventures of the News Reel Cameraman. 183
American Graffiti 22
An American in Paris 123
Another New Paramount Talkartoon 163
Another New Popeye Comedy 168
Arsene Lupin 59
Assassin of Youth 217
Atom Man vs. Superman 348
The Awful Tooth 229

The Babbling Book 244
Babes in Arms 113
Babes in the Goods 143
Bad Girls Go to Hell 220
Be Human 166
Believe It or Not 142
Bells of Rosarita 331
The Bells of St. Mary's 134
The Big Game 44
The Big Shot 77
A Bill of Divorcement 60
Black cast lobby cards (30) 351
The Blob 209
Blonde Crazy 56
The Blue Dahlia .64, 71, 93
Bogart lobby cards (10) 90
Bosko and the Pirates 160
Boxing Posters (6) 39
The Brasher Doubloon 74
Bridal Bail 257
The Bride Walks Out 138
Broadway Ballyhoo 99
Broadway Brevities 104
Broadway Musketeers 129
Bugs in Love 265
Building Winners 34
Bullitt 15
Bus Stop 291

Cafe Metropole 62
Calcutta 66
Came the Brawn 230
The Canyon of Light 251
Captain Kidd's Treasure .148
Carefree 109
Casa Manana Revue 147
Casey at the Mets 37
Charlie Chan at the Race Track 84
Charlie Chan lobby cards (7) 95
Cinderella 279
Circus Days 155
Cocaine 218
Counsellor-At-Law 58
Court of Human Relations 189
Creature From the Black Lagoon 200
The Crowd Roars 41
Cubby Bear 154

A Damsel in Distress 111
The Daredevil 249
David Friedman one-sheets (4) 221
Davy Crockett, King of the Wild Frontier. 282

Deep in the Heart of Texas 321
The Deer Hunter 19
Disneyland After Dark 288
Double Indemnity 68
Double or Nothing 103
Dracula Prince of Darkness 7
Dumbo 269

East of Borneo 368
Easter Parade 125, 126
Eight and a Half 3
The Endless Summer 23
Enter the Dragon 11
The Everlasting Whisper 247
The Explorer 153

The Falcon Takes Over 88
Fantasia 270
Faster Pussycat! Kill! Kill! 222, 223
Fate's Fathead 241
Ferdinand the Bull 271
The Fight Never Ends 352
The Flaming Frontier 252
Flight to Mars 198, 212
Footlight Serenade 117
For a Few Dollars More .342
For Me and My Gal 114
Forbidden 51
The Fountainhead 82
Frankenstein Meets the Wolf Man 192
From Russia With Love 10
Frontier Pony Express 326
Fun and Fancy Free 277

Gags and Gals 187
Gala Day at Disneyland .287
Gene Autry lobby cards (8) 337
Giant 302
The Glass Key 65
Going My Way 133
Goldfinger 9
The Great Escape 13
Grips, Grunts and Groans 313
Gun Crazy 92

A Hard Day's Night 4
Harlem Rides the Range 355
Headlines of 25 Years 184
Heart of the Golden West 327
Hearts Divided 137
Hello, Frisco, Hello 120
Hercules 12
Hi-Neighbor 228
Hidden Gold 246
High Noon 338
High Plains Drifter 344
High Speed 42
Holiday Inn 119
Hollywood on Parade 304
Horror of Dracula 210
The Horror of Party Beach 214
The House of Frankenstein 193
How to Be a Detective .239

The Hustler 17
I am a Fugitive From a Chain Gang 47
I Heard 162
I Married A Witch 131
I Wanted Wings 130
I'll Take Vanilla 240
If This Isn't Love 256
In-Laws are Out 259
Invasion of the Body Snatchers 205
Invasion of the Saucer-Men 204
The Iron Horse 253
It Came From Outer Space 203, 213
It Happened One Night 57

James Dean one-sheets (3) 300
The Jazz Singer 106
Jesse James at Bay 329
Jezebel 136, 140
Juke Joint 360
The Jungle Book 369

The Kid Brother 227
Knee-Deep in Music 254
Krazy Spooks 152

La Dolce Vita 1, 2
La Savate 309
Lady and the Tramp 283
Le Mans 16
Leave Her to Heaven 75
Left Handed Law 318
Let's All Sing Like the Birdies Sing 169
Lifeboat 96
The Lone Ranger 341
Love Happy 292
Love in the Rough 35
Love Me Tender 298

Macao 83
Magic Carpet of Movietone 182
The Magnificent Seven 14
Major Bowes Amateur Parade 260
Make Mine Music 276
Making Friends 165
Manhattan 24
The March of Time 262
Marihuana 216
Marijuana 215
Marilyn Monroe lobby cards (15) 296
Melody Master Bands 102
Melody Ranch 336
Melody Time 278
Men Without Law 317
Merrie Melodies (c.1934) 173
The Merrie Melodies (c.1932) 175
Merry X-Mas and a Happy New Year 234
Mickey Mouse (1932) 263
Mickey Mouse (1935) 264
Mickey's Covered Wagon 235
Mickey's Disguise 232
Midnight Cowboy 18
Mighty Joe Young 371
Million Dollar Melody 185